ASPECTS OF WAKEFIELD 2

ASPECTS *of* WAKEFIELD

DISCOVERING LOCAL HISTORY 2

Edited by
Kate Taylor

Series Editor
Brian Elliott

Wharncliffe Publishing

First Published in 1999 by
Wharncliffe Publishing
an imprint of
Pen and Sword Books Limited,
47 Church Street, Barnsley,
South Yorkshire. S70 2AS

Copyright © Wharncliffe Publishing 1999

For up-to-date information on other titles produced under the Wharncliffe imprint, please telephone or write to:

Wharncliffe Publishing
FREEPOST
47 Church Street
Barnsley
South Yorkshire S70 2BR
Telephone (24 hours): 01226 - 734555

ISBN: 1-871647-68-1

A CIP catalogue record of this book is available from the British Library

Cover illustration: Upper Westgate, 1896, by Louis Grimshaw. *Courtesy of Wakefield Art Gallery*

Printed in Great Britain by
Redwood Books, Trowbridge, Wiltshire

£1-50

CONTENTS

INTRODUCTION

by Kate Taylor

This second volume of *Aspects of Wakefield* reflects the research interests of a very varied group of people. Yet there are a quite surprising number of links between one essay and another so that at times it has been difficult to decide quite where to place the illustrations. Should the picture of Walton Hall have been used to illustrate John Goodchild's reference to the world's first nature reserve rather than to show where, between 1942 and 1967, many people who will read these pages were born? Portobello House, the home of some of the dyeing Holdsworth family, about whom John Goodchild writes, was bought by Wakefield Corporation for the development of the council estate which is the subject of Angela Petyt's essay. Wakefield's magnificent Corn Exchange was the venue for a great Methodist celebration referred to by Paul Dawson in his study of West Parade, and for social events noted in Anthony Dawson's account of the Wakefield Rifle Volunteers.

The essays reflect the industrial, commercial, social and religious life of the Wakefield district. K O M Golisti shows how Wakefield capitalised on the development of gas as an illuminant. Keith Wainwright, who wrote about coal-mining entrepreneur Bram Pashley in the first volume of *Aspects of Wakefield*, writes here about a Crigglestone colliery and tramway. Norman Ellis provides recollections of the shops and the itinerant traders serving the growing Outwood community in the 1930s. Peter Wood's account of Walter Hampson, of the Clock Almanack, refers, inter alia, to the Normanton dialect poet's excursions both in England and abroad. Was participation in the activities of the rifle volunteers a social activity? Certainly Anthony Dawson shows that the volunteers' field days could be an exciting entertainment for the wider community. And, of course, they had dances as well as drills!

The remarkable Wood family, the subject of study by Anthony Petyt, were farmers but one of their number became distinguished nationally - and even internationally, as a singer. Music-making is the raison d'etre of Crofton's Silver Band but their funds have always been dependent on social events from coffee mornings to beetle drives and, again, dances.

Some of these essays reflect the grimmer – or certainly grimier – aspects of local life. David Scriven, a contributor to the first Wakefield *Aspects* again focuses on Ossett but in this volume shows the impact of the First World War. Angela Petyt remarks on the slum conditions and the terrible outbreaks of disease which led – eventually – to the development of high-quality local authority housing schemes. Much earlier housing schemes for the disadvantaged are the focus of Sue Lambert's study of the Frieston and Sagar almshouse charities.

Wakefield's handsome West Parade Chapel, the subject of extensive and continuing research by Paul Dawson, was designed as a complement to a very different, handsome Georgian housing scheme in South Parade.

Whilst I am grateful to all those who have contributed their work to this volume, I should just say how particularly encouraging it has been to find both enthusiasm and developing research skills in the Dawson twins who will be barely nineteen at the time of this book's publication. In selecting material for this volume I have been 'spoilt for choice' and some excellent submissions have had to be rejected, or at least retained for a possible third volume.

Meanwhile, under the immediate nurturing of Mike Parsons, the *Aspects* series is growing rapidly both in the number of volumes relating to individual places (there is now an *Aspects of Barnsley 5!*) and in its geographical scope with new volumes on *Aspects of Birmingham, Blackburn, Hull* and the *Yorkshire Coast*. For the continuing success of this series we continue to need new writers. Anyone interested in contributing to a third *Aspects of Wakefield* is most warmly invited to contact me, Kate Taylor, c/o Wharncliffe Publishing Ltd, 47 Church Street, Barnsley, S70 2AS.

Finally I must thank not only the indefatigable and always good–humoured Mike Parsons and Brian Elliott, the general editor of the series for their support and advice, but the other staff at Wharncliffe, especially Jon Wilkinson for his attractive design and typesetting.

1. WAKEFIELD BY GASLIGHT

by K O M Golisti

THE CREATION OF A LIGHT without a wick may be credited to the Reverend Dr John Clayton, rector of Crofton, near Wakefield, from 1687 to 1699 who about 1684, following a series of logical and carefully executed experiments, was the first to place on record that the distillation of coal, in a closed vessel, produced an inflammable gas (referred to by Clayton as a spirit of coal) that could be collected and stored, in bladders, for future use. He was to write:

> *...and when I had a mind to divert strangers or friends I have taken one of these bladders and pricking a hole thereon with a pin and compressing gently the bladder near the flame of a candle till it once took fire it would continue flaming till all the spirit was compressed out of the bladder...*[1]

In 1771 an Act of Parliament established the Wakefield Street Commissioners for the purpose of repairing and draining the streets. In 1796 and again in 1816 Acts of Parliament were obtained to extend the Commissioners' powers for the *better lighting and watching of the town of Wakefield*, authorising the cost to be a charge on the owners and occupiers of property; that rated below £4 and the mills of Sir Thomas Pilkington were exempt. Lighting was by means of oil lamps.

The invention of a new light, from coal gas, at the end of the eighteenth century brought major benefits, ending man's dependence on daylight, with obvious implications for the social life of the community and having a dramatic impact on industry, making night work possible for the first time with a safer, superior and cheaper illuminant.

It was to the talents of a Scot, William Murdock(h), that we in Britain owe the first instance of gas distilled from coal becoming a practical and economic illuminant and to him must be awarded the merit of being the first to devise and arrange apparatus for the practical production and utilisation of gas. All historians agree that in 1792 he lit his house in Redruth in Cornwall from a piped supply of coal gas.

The concept of a public supply of gas, produced at a central location and then piped to the premises of those who wished to use it, via pipes buried in the streets, came from a German, Frederich Albrect Winzer (later anglicised to Winsor). His energy obtained sufficient public support in 1810 to finance the world's first gas company, the London and Westminster Gas Light and Coke Company. Obtaining incorporated status in 1812, it became known as the 'chartered' Company, or Gas Light and Coke Company. Its Beckton gasworks, the location of the Millenium Dome, became the largest in the world.

There was a demonstration of gas lighting at the Old Assembly Rooms in Wakefield in 1806 by Dr Staincliffe. The *Wakefield Star* advertised an:

opportunity of viewing some simple and practical apparatus for lighting rooms by the clarified product of common coal. Many experiments have been lately given by Dr. Staincliffe in the most populous parts of this liberal and enlightened district. It cannot but be pleasing to every rank to learn that the apparatus has been brought by Dr. 'S' to high perfection and that dwelling houses, warehouses, shops and factory may now be lighted at an expense 100 times less than wax candles. The light being at the same time both intense and grateful to the eye.[2]

It is important to note that a cotton spinner, Henry Lodge of Sowerby Bridge (then a mere hamlet) had the previous December installed a gas works in order to light his mill - the earliest recorded practical use of gas lighting in Yorkshire.

We next learn in April 1818 of apparatus claimed as suitable for producing gas for domestic use:

the simplest form of retort can be obtained from an old kettle or glue pot with a tin cover, half full of coals and placed on the fire so that the bottom is always in contact with the red coals, which will distil enough gas to burn for three or four hours at the end of a thin tube which has a curvature, being four foot long and half an inch in diameter, extending from the mouth of the retort. For this kind of domestic light it is necessary to purify the gas by passing it through a vessel four foot by two inches square, filled with tow that has been oiled and well greased, it being necessary to change the tow not more than once a month. When not in use this vessel may be ornamental and hung over the mantle piece every night.[3]

Not long after this gas lighting was installed in a Wakefield mill. Henry Clarkson, referring to 1820, states:

> *...the small scribbling and carding mill in the Alverthorpe Road which belonged to my father was the only one in town employed in woollen manufacture. It was the first mill lighted by gas for my father made his own some years previous to the town being lighted in that way, and I well remember the number of people who collected round the mill to see the wonderful new light.*[4]

Unfortunately there is no information as to the precise date, or which of the relatively few engineers installing gas plants was employed in design and erection of the apparatus.

Gas was also produced by 1822 by a Mr Clay, proprietor of billiard rooms in Wakefield, whose wife learnt the hard way that searching for a gas escape with a lighted flame invited disaster:

> *A most unfortunate accident occurred on the 29th at the Billiard Rooms in Wakefield, which has been for some time lighted with gas from a small private apparatus belonging to Mr. Clay, the proprietor of the rooms. Some obstruction having taken place in the regular supply to the burner, the wife of the proprietor took a lighted candle to see what was the matter; the resultant explosion set fire to her clothes and severely burnt her.*[5]

How were the streets of Wakefield lit in days gone by? Surviving records suggest indifferently. The preamble to the *Street Commissioners' 1816 Act* states:

> *...it would be of great benefit to the inhabitants and all persons resorting to and travelling through Wakefield if the streets were properly lighted and watched.*

A meeting of influential residents was held on 6 August 1821 to discuss the use of gas for illumination. It was followed by another meeting, presided over by the Reverend Samuel Sharp, vicar of Wakefield, when the propriety of forming a gas light company was discussed. There appears to have been little difficulty in procuring finance as within a month some 98 individuals, thirteen of them women, had indicated that they were prepared to become subscribers. Was the incentive that stimulated investment public service, or private gain?

It is important to recognise that well into the second half of the nineteenth century the sole market for gas was illumination and that, coke apart, there was no significant revenue from the variety of residual products resulting from the carbonisation of coal.

The evolution of the Wakefield Gas Light Company falls into fairly well defined periods. Until 1880 its dominant role was as a supplier of light, having no competitor comparable in cost and convenience. The next period, up to the First World War (1914) was marked by increasing competition from electricity in the lighting field, and a growing use of gas for cooking and heating. From 1919 to nationalisation (1949) increasing competition from electricity led to further emphasis on the use of gas as a fuel.

The writer proposes to take the starting point of a public supply of gas at Wakefield as Saturday, 6 October 1821, the date when the subscribers were invited to a meeting in the Court House presided over by Reverend Sharp, when it was resolved that:

> *It was expedient for a gas light company, with the title the Wakefield Gas Light and Coke Company be formed, obtaining the approval of Parliament to manufacture and supply gas light into Wakefield and that the present subscribers be its members.*

The decision to operate within the protection of Parliament suggests apprehension at the speculative nature of the venture: an act of Parliament limited liability to the amount of the investment; operating as a co-partnership creditors could claim on the personal wealth of the proprietors.

The *Wakefield Gas Act*, which received royal assent on 3 April 1822, shortened the name to the Wakefield Gas Light Company. Amending acts or orders were introduced in 1847, 1856, 1877, 1922 and 1943, increasing the authorised level of capital and sanctioning additional powers and responsibilities. It was legislation in 1948 that obliterated the company, along with all other gas undertakings in the country.

The sum of £12,500, raised by the issue of £25 shares, with powers to borrow up to 25 per cent of the issued capital, was deemed adequate to establish the undertaking. To ensure that no single individual obtained control, the maximum holding was limited to twenty shares. It is interesting to note that the four shares of one original subscriber, George Oldroyd, remained in the family's portfolio until 1943 when they were acquired by the United Kingdom Gas Corporation who obtained control of the company.

There was the right to supply gas into an area not exceeding 3000 yards radius of the market cross. By the centenary year gas was supplied into an area extending eight miles at its longest length and three miles at its broadest width.

Two basic problems faced the nascent company - finding a location for the gasworks and finding a man with sufficient

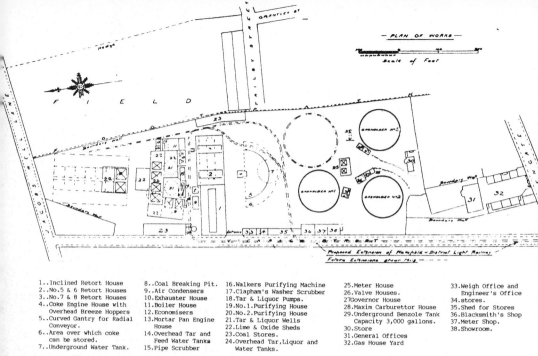

Figure 1. Plan of the Wakefield Gaslight Company's premises in 1900.
British Gas archives, Partington.

1..Inclined Retort House	8..Coal Breaking Pit.	16.Walkers Purifying Machine	25.Meter House	33.Weigh Office and
2..No.5 & 6 Retort Houses	9..Air Condensers	17.Clapham's Washer Scrubber	26.Valve Houses.	Engineer's Office
3..No.7 & 8 Retort Houses	10.Exhauster House	18.Tar & Liquor Pumps.	27Governor House	34.stores.
4..Coke Engine House with	11.Boiler House	19.No.1.Purifying House	28.Maxim Carburettor House	35.Shed for Stores
Overhead Breeze Hoppers	12.Economisers	20.No.2.Purifying House	29.Underground Benzole Tank	36.Blacksmith's Shop
5..Curved Gantry for Radial	13.Mortar Pan Engine	21.Tar & Liquor Wells	Capacity 3,000 gallons.	37.Meter Shop.
Conveyor.	House	22.Lime & Oxide Sheds	30.Store	38.Showroom.
6..Area over which coke	14.Overhead Tar and	23.Coal Stores.	31.General Offices	
can be stored.	Feed Water Tanks	24.Overhead Tar,Liquor and	32.Gas House Yard	
7..Underground Water Tank.	15.Pipe Scrubber	Water Tanks.		

knowledge of gas works construction and gas manufacture. The industry was new and there were few engineers with the requisite skills. The promoters were to experience a 'nimby' culture: whilst the influential were quite prepared to accept the physical and economic benefits of gas lighting, few wished to have a gas works in their vicinity. The magistrates objected to the preferred location, at the bottom of Westgate, on the grounds of its being a nuisance to the prison. Three other sites, on the Ings, at the bottom of New Street, and on Westgate Common, were rejected for one reason or another.

Finally an acre of land known as Oliver Ings, north of Warrengate, approximately a third of a mile, and on the lee side of the town centre (where the market for gas lighting was located) was rented. During 1832 the land and mineral rights were purchased from Thomas Bedford at a cost of £2,087 14s. One would need to multiply the figure by some 200 to find an equivalent value today. Further land was acquired as the demand for gas dictated expansion of the gas works (Figure 1).[6]

Finding a competent engineer was not to prove difficult. One of the initial subscribers was John Malam, who had taken four shares, a man who, with his brothers James and George played a significant role in the development of gas lighting not only in England and Ireland but also on the continent. James became the pioneer of gaslighting in Sweden.[7]

Figure 2. Westgate flanked by gaslamps towards the end of the nineteenth century. *Wakefield Historical Publications*

John Malam's proposals appear to have been accepted without quibble (at least nothing survives to suggest otherwise) for the design, procurement and installation of the specialist apparatus, together with obtaining stone, bricks, ironwork and roofing materials, the engagement of local craftsmen and labourers for the range of buildings that comprised the gasworks, together with the gas distribution network, and putting the whole into operation. He was paid £7,302 9s 1d. It is of interest to note that in the centenary year carbonising wages amounted to £5,302.

Clearly there were no problems associated with procurement of the specialist apparatus from Thorncliffe Ironworks on schedule or with the construction of the buildings as work was sufficiently advanced for gas to be produced some four months after the laying of the foundation stone on 18 September 1822 by G Teale. There is an element of uncertainty about the actual start of gas making. Some sources say 23, others 30 January 1823.[8] Gas production ceased on 24 January 1953, when the retort house fell silent. It was no longer a financially viable production unit.

The Street Commissioners were eager to negotiate a lighting contract. The gentle golden glow from 104 street lamps lit several of the more important streets at the end of January 1823. In spite of indifferent weather, a large crowd turned out for the occasion with the workmen parading behind a band of music. By modern standards the light would be dim and diffused, but to our forefathers it would be prodigious illumination.[9] It was the practice in the nineteenth century, and well into the twentieth, for street lamps to be lit for specified periods of time, and not throughout the night and year as is the practice today. In 1846 the only lamp lit all night was that outside the Post Office. Important thoroughfares were lit the longest and other roads and alleys for much shorter periods. This piecemeal arrangement included an economy measure of not lighting the gas lamps during the 'light of the moon', the term for several nights either side of the full moon (Figure 2). The total earnings of the eight lamplighters employed during the 1855-56 lighting season amounted to £192 5s 7d., the most highly-paid receiving a weekly wage of 12s. Each man was responsible for 72 lamps, placed at an average of 60 yards apart in those streets that were illuminated; all had to be lit or extinguished within one hour. When street lighting resumed in 1945 following wartime restrictions clockwork mechanism was fitted to each of the 1,200 street lamps the Wakefield Corporation contracted for. Street lighting by gas continued up to and after nationalisation.

Unfortunately details of the mains laid by Mr Malam have not survived. It is not unreasonable to assume mainlaying was restricted to those streets along which the 104 lamps had been placed. The rating assessment of 1858 indicates that the company paid rates on some 30,000 yards of various diameter mains. When the company emerged from the hostilities of the Second World War gas was supplied through 135 miles of mains. The high level of mining activity resulted in land subsidence and a high incidence of fractures of the cast-iron main that formed the gas distribution system. The company developed considerable expertise in damage limitation, with the judicious use of steel pipes and advanced main-laying techniques.

Whether through democracy or

Figure 3. Notice issued by the Wakefield Gaslight Company in 1844. *British Gas archives, Partington*

Further Reduction in the Price of Gas.

WAKEFIELD GAS-LIGHT COMPANY.

THE COMMITTEE OF THE WAKEFIELD GAS-LIGHT COMPANY give Notice to their Consumers by Meter—that from and after the 1st day of *July*, 1844, the following will be the **Nett** Charge for Gas, upon **each Half-Year's Account,** ending the 30th *June*, and the 31st *December*, when the consumption shall be as follows :—

				s.	d.	
Under	......	20,000 feet	6	8	℔ 1000 cubic ft.
20,000	and not exceeding	50,000	.. 6	4	"
50,000	"	100,000	.. 6	0	"
100,000	"	150,000	.. 5	8	"
150,000	"	200,000	.. 5	4	"
	200,000 feet and upwards	5	0		"

The Consumers will be allowed to provide their own Meters, " *on sending them to the Works for trial and inspection ;*" or they will be furnished by the Company at the following Charge of Interest *per Annum,* viz.

						s.	d.
2 Lights	.	.	.	.	.	2	6
5 Do.	.	.	.	.	.	3	6
10 Do.	.	.	.	.	.	5	0
20 Do.	.	.	.	.	.	7	6
30 Do.	.	.	.	.	.	10	0
50 Do.	.	.	.	.	.	15	0
80 Do.	.	.	.	.	.	21	0
100 Do.	.	.	.	.	.	30	0

If a Meter (from being out of order) should not mark correctly the quantity of Gas consumed, the Consumer shall pay after the rate indicated by the Meter, when in good repair.

WAKEFIELD GAS OFFICE, *June*, 1844.

Regulations of the Wakefield Gas Ligh' Company.

Extract from Gas Works Clauses Amendment Act, 34 & 35 Vict., Cap. 41; A.D. 1871.

1—No consumer shall connect any Meter with *any pipe* through which Gas is supplied by the Undertakers to such Meter or disconnect any Meter from any such pipe, unless he shall have given to the Undertakers not less than twenty-four hours notice in writing of his intention so to do. And if any person acts in contravention of this Section he shall be liable for each offence to a penalty not exceeding 40/-.

2—Any person removing from or to premises supplied with gas by this Company without giving immediate notice of such removal, is rendered liable for any gas consumed by the next or previous tenant during the then current half-year.

3—If at any time it be ascertained that the Meter has not registered the quantity of gas consumed, the manager has power to estimate the consumption during the period of incorrect registration and to charge for the same. The Gas Company will not be responsible for any damage from explosions arising from defective Fittings in the interior of Buildings.

4—Service pipes from the Street Main to the face of the building. area, yard or garden, are laid by the Company free of expense, to the extent of thirty feet, beyond that distance at the expense of the consumer, but service pipes. taps and joints on all private property whatever, whether gardens, areas, yards or buildings, are charged to the consumer, and are his own property (and must be kept in good repair), and are expected to be paid for as soon as completed.

Instructions to Consumers.

1—All premises are supplied by a main tap, which will be found near the meter, attached to the service pipe which supplies the premises,—this tap should be frequently turned to secure its always being fit for use.

2—When any quantity of gas has escaped, turn off the supply at the main tap until a gas-fitter can be found to examine the gas fittings. Open the doors and upper sashes of the windows, not only where the gas has escaped, but also in the adjoining rooms and passages.

3—Sliding chandeliers require an occasional supply of water, which is to be poured into the cup at the top of the chandelier. These chandeliers should always be pushed up during the night, or when the apartment is left for any length of time.

4—Never enter a room with a light, when an escape of gas is suspected.

5—In times of severe frost meters should be well covered, or inconvenience may arise from freezing of the water, and consequent stoppage of the gas.

6—When there is a deficiency of gas, or a jumping of the lights, it should be first ascertained whether the whole of the lights or a part only are affected,—if a part only, application should be made to a fitter; but if the whole, to the Company.   **W. H. Milnes, Printer.**

Figure 4. The regulations of the Wakefield Gaslight Company, 1871. *British Gas archives, Partington*

friction, for several years the office of chairman rotated between several individuals. However that changed following the election of the surgeon, William Statter, to the Board in June 1828. He became chairman in 1838 holding the office until his death, aged 89, in 1896. He was succeeded by his son, Dr W A Statter (elected a director in 1892) who retained the office until his death on 22 November 1914. In recognition of Mr Statter's fifty-plus years' service, shareholders in 1896 voted £200 for his portrait to be painted in oils. It is not known whether he ever sat for it.

William Statter became the foremost non-technical gas man in the West Riding, being chairman of five gas companies and either on the board, or an influential shareholder in many others. He was closely involved with the vicar of St Andrew's, Wakefield, Reverend William Renwick Bowditch, in his patented gas-purification process. Bowditch, who wrote a gas text book, made significant improvements to gas lighting technology.

Originally gas was sold by contract, at a fixed sum of money for specified burners in use for a defined period of time during the evening of a six-day week. This clearly indicated that the market was for those who did not use a light on the Sabbath - shops and the like.

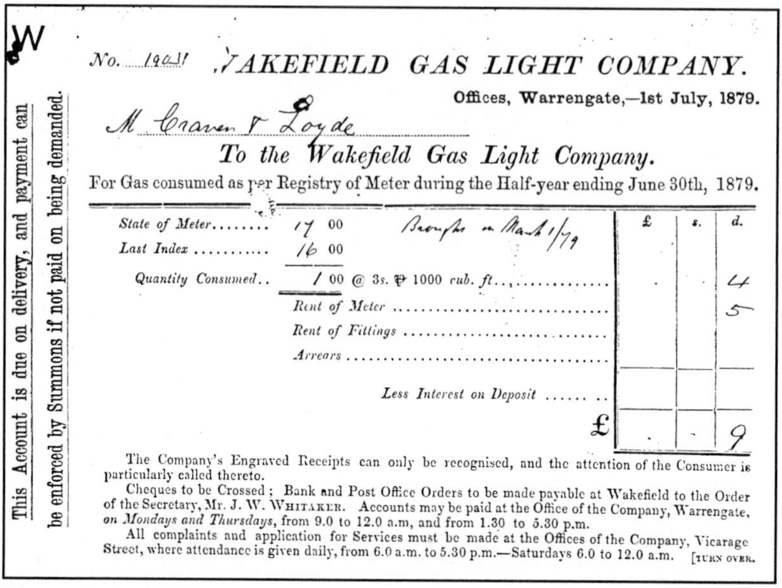

This Account is due on delivery, and payment can be enforced by Summons if not paid on being demanded.

No. 19031 WAKEFIELD GAS LIGHT COMPANY.

Offices, Warrengate,—1st July, 1879.

M Craven & Loyde

To the Wakefield Gas Light Company.

For Gas consumed as per Registry of Meter during the Half-year ending June 30th, 1879.

			£	s.	d.
State of Meter........	17 00				
Last Index	16 00				
Quantity Consumed..	1 00 @ 3s. ℔ 1000 cub. ft..............				4
	Rent of Meter				5
	Rent of Fittings				
	Arrears				
	Less Interest on Deposit				
		£	.	-	9

The Company's Engraved Receipts can only be recognised, and the attention of the Consumer is particularly called thereto.

Cheques to be Crossed; Bank and Post Office Orders to be made payable at Wakefield to the Order of the Secretary, Mr. J. W. WHITAKER. Accounts may be paid at the Office of the Company, Warrengate, *on Mondays and Thursdays*, from 9.0 to 12.0 a.m, and from 1.30 to 5.30 p.m.

All complaints and application for Services must be made at the Offices of the Company, Vicarage Street, where attendance is given daily, from 6.0 a.m. to 5.30 p.m.—Saturdays 6.0 to 12.0 a.m. [TURN OVER.

Figure 5. An invoice for a very modest consumption of gas in 1879. Craven and Loyd were builders with premises in Bank Street. *British Gas archives, Partington.*

There were special arrangements for those who wished to have light on Sundays. The contract system had the advantage of payment being made in advance of consumption, thus providing capital to finance subsequent activities; it also reduced the incidence of bad debts. Anyone who wished to have volumetric measurement had to provide their own meter (after approval of the type) and were charged 12s per 1,000 cubic feet of gas. This sum may not have been exploitation but a reflection of harsh economic facts; nevertheless such a price placed the product beyond the reach of the mass of market potential (Figures 3-5).

Human nature being what it is, there was abuse: during May 1830 warning notices were displayed around town warning that:

such people who consume gas beyond the time contracted for would be fined.

A tea dealer was before the magistrates in January 1832 for burning gas in his shop between 8.00am and 9.00am when his contract allowed him to use gas lighting only from dusk to 9.00pm. He was fined 15s plus costs. The company asked that the fine be paid to the Wakefield Dispensary. The incident hints at the hours shopkeepers were trading.

The directors would have been acting rationally in showing preference to prominent industrialists. It was essential that their custom was secured at a price which forestalled those with financial resources installing their own gas-making facilities. There were nonetheless to be some few private manufacturers of gas in Wakefield but whilst several were to provide gas for lighting streets in their immediate vicinity, there is nothing to suggest they sought to maximise on their investment by providing a public supply of gas.

Within a few years of its foundation, twenty-seven mills and twenty-six workshops were being supplied by the Wakefield Gas Company. As they were vulnerable to trade cycles an alternative market was developed. For reasons that have slipped into oblivion, it was not the domestic market that was targeted but inns, then as today popular with the British working male population; the publican, anxious to improve his premises, introduced gas lighting. By 1846 some 106 inns and beer houses were illuminated by gas. Gas was also supplied to 377 shops, warehouses and malt kilns, 75 offices and surgeries, and 14 places of worship. There were only 115 lights in 82 private houses.[10]

The interest of Wakefield Borough Council in the gas business is well documented. However the local authority was never able to get sufficient support from the ratepayers to buy the company. In 1884 the Wakefield Trade Association was urging that every monopoly should be brought under the control of the Corporation. When the purchase of the Borough Market and the Gas Company was under consideration, Mr Briggs, president of the Chamber of Commerce, pointed out that purchase would result in higher rates. A Mr Carter was of the opinion that the Market should be bought but that the Gas Company would be too expensive. His opinion held for the remainder of the era of private gas.

Initially there were few full-time workers. The key employees were stokers. Their work was long (twelve hour shifts) and arduous. Nevertheless it was superior to that of the coalminer. Consequently there was a pool of men ready and willing to fill any vacancy, the basic numbers being increased as necessary to meet the seasonal demand for gas. The arbitrator at the 1858 rating appeal was told that the number of stokers varied between sixteen in mid winter and four in summer.

A generalised description of associated activities may help to provide an insight into the working of the retort house where the length of the retort was between seven and ten feet:

The filling and wheeling of a barrow (containing from 1.5 to 2 cwts) of blended and sized coal from the coal store or stack to the proximity of the retort setting. It was the responsibility of the stoker to carefully open the closure door of the retort, immediately igniting the escaping gas (to avoid the risk of explosion); the next job was to clear deposited carbon and tar from the ascension pipe (that took gas out of the retort) by using an 'augar' of about six feet in length.

The removal of the incandescent mass of coke that lay on the bottom of the retort was achieved by the stoker pushing an iron rake to the back of the mass and pulling it forward so that it fell into an iron barrow that had previously been placed below the open retort mouth. The coke was then 'quenched' with water. These activities resulted in a mixture of heat, dust, smoke and gas, in short a most unpleasant and unhealthy working environment. Protecting the face by the best means that could be thought of, the barrow was wheeled into the yard to deposit the coke.

The stoker, standing in front of the empty retort, began to shovel coal into the retort, the first shovelful going to its back, subsequent shovelfuls fell slightly short of its predecessor until the whole length was filled, leaving a gap of some six inches above the coal layer. Whilst all this was taking place, crude gas poured out which the closing of the retort door stopped. The commencement of the carbonising cycle.

The increase in demand for gas was accompanied by an increase in the length of the retort (up to twenty feet) resulting in the shovel technique being replaced by a semi-cylinder of metal as long as the retort (the scoop) in which the coal charge was placed. Its insertion into the retort, and rotation, enabled the coal to be deposited in a single operation.

From the earliest of days, coke found a ready market, often realising a price at or near the original price of the coal. One of the principal markets was the malt kiln. In 1902 the chairman, in his attempt to explain why the usual 11 per cent dividend had not been earned, referred to:

the high cost of coal and the fall in the price of tar, but the main reason was the 'arsenic in the beer' scare which had at one blow deprived the company of the sale of coke for malting purposes, which hitherto had been their chief market.[11]

With the twentieth century, overseas markets were developed. A cryptic entry in the minute book tells of a failed export: '*the coke for Copenhagen off*'. During 1943 coke sales realised £25,537, and the cost of coal was £46,315. The total income that year was £418,007.

The development of the chemical industry and the discovery of

Figure 6. The offices of the Wakefield Gaslight Company, in Warrengate. *Kate Taylor*

synthetic dyestuff opened up new markets, providing a substantial if variable income, during 1877 amounting to £5,771 (income from gas £17,650). Tar, an embarrassment during the pioneer years, was subsequently sold on annual contracts to chemical manufacturers. During 1926 the West Riding County Council purchased upwards of 27,000 gallons at 5d per gallon, ex.works, or 5.5d delivered within a ten-mile radius of the gas works, delivery being made with a recently acquired Sentinel lorry.

Industrial relations in the nineteenth century Wakefield Gas Light Company were hierarchical with the manager (sometimes referred to as secretary) being seen as the master to whom respect was due, difficult to examine in detail, seldom defined - basically an ad hoc response to immediate problems (Figure 6). Once a worker proved reliable, honest and industrious, family members were employed. This form of nepotism applied to all levels of the labour force.

The Wakefield Gas Light Company was to receive extended service from both individuals and families. The longest family association was that of the Milsoms. The first of that name, William, commenced his duties as gas maker (manager) in April 1824; others were employed in a variety of jobs for upwards of 150 years. Norman Milsom had given forty-nine years service when he died in February 1971.

There were other families. During Bernard Glover's last year at work (1969) he was awarded the British Empire Medal, retiring with fifty-two years service. His grandfather Joe had a long serving career; his father, another Joe, achieved fifty years. William Duce retired in 1969 after fifty-two years, having started as an apprentice fitter, earning 4s (20p) a week. He was shop steward for upwards of thirty years. His brother Fred worked for fifty years in the industry; two of their uncles were employees.

As the nineteenth century progressed, from the harsh reality of the cash nexus emerged gratuities. In February 1848 shareholders voted the directors, engineer, manager and solicitor £5 each. Workmen got 5s (25p) each. The chairman was frequently voted an honorarium. In 1909 Foreman T K Milsom was paid £1 for every million cubic feet of gas by which he reduced the 'unaccounted for gas' level. In 1916 W H Obell, who retired in 1945 after 37 years service, was paid £10 for his patented modification to the coal-handling plant.

Following injury at work or sickness, there were awards at the directors' discretion. When employees set up their own sick fund the directors made an annual donation. Hospitals at Buxton and Southport were to receive donations following the admittance of an employee. There were contributions to the popular works trip, taken on alternative Saturday. Some £200 was contributed to the final trip in 1948.

There were few of the well-provided shareholders who gave much thought to employees. One who did was G Moorhouse, Mayor in 1884. At the general meeting in 1876 he asked that £300 of the £10,000 profit be allocated to

> long time servants who had contributed, by their efforts, to the creation of this money.

The motion was not approved. In 1879 he voiced his opinion of the directors, who had reduced the wages of the stokers from 30s (£1. 50p) to 27s (£1. 35p) per week whilst the manager had been awarded substantial increases, and a 1 per cent increase in dividends. Chairman Statter who, in addition to director's fees received £100 pa considered:

> These workpeople were paid very handsomely for work which did not require any special training and he believed they were well satisfied.

Another of the assembled proprietors was of the opinion that

> ...for the men to be better paid could result in there being less devotion to their duties.

The ensuing debate was well ventilated in the newspaper. Shortly afterwards the press were excluded from meetings.

The introduction in 1895 of the pre-payment (coin in slot) meter created a new class of employee termed 'auto collector'. Initially this form of budgetary control was introduced into the homes of the more prosperous (who wished to know how much gas was being used in the kitchen) or artisan rather than the working class. However, the trading environment demanded that the customer base be broadened, resulting in their introduction into tenement property.

As the head of the household left for work early in the morning, to ensure he had a hot meal, or at least a hot drink, a small breakfast griller was supplied with these meters (another innovation was a boiling ring). As no money changed hands it was thought they were free; of course they were not, the capital and other costs being recovered by adjusting the quantity of gas obtained for the coin (one penny) inserted in the meter.

The entry of the auto-collector into the homes of gas users could be an adventure, occasions when the visit was welcomed because once the pile of coins had been added up, the housewife got what she called 'returns', perhaps half a dozen or so pennies, a considerable sum in the hard days of the 1930s, for example. As the rebate varied, there were occasions when nothing was returned, resulting in disappointment and even allegation of 'sticky fingers'. There were also unpleasant times: the meter had been raided and there was no alternative but to take all the particulars possible and prepare a report for the manager, for appropriate action to be decided.

During the period June to December 1902 there were three auto collectors whose salaries ranged between £65 and £80 a year. That half year they took over a million pennies (240 to the £1) from 3,513 coin meters. With three pennies weighing an ounce, and no transport, the duties could not be considered light. Then there was the responsibility of carrying the money through the streets on foot, followed by the adding up of coins and reconciling their value with the records.

There were three other collectors who visited customers for the quarterly collection of over 5,700 accounts. Their salaries ranged from £85 to £100. The dedication these men gave to their duties may be noted from the level of bad debts in their districts. In June to December 1906 they were £9 5s 3d., £5 14s 2d., and £8 17s 2d.

Following the reduction of working hours in the retort house, from twelve to eight in July 1913, the hours of non shift workers were reduced to 52 hours a week. On Monday there was a late start at

7.00am, Tuesday to Friday 6.00am to 5.00pm, and Saturday 6.00pm to noon. The wage of a labourer for a full week's work was 26s (130p). When overtime was demanded it was at the standard rate. By 1931 hours had been reduced to 47 and pay increased to £52s 7d. The 44-hour (five and a half day) week was introduced on 4 May 1947. Shift workers, who on balance worked an eight-hour shift, received a compensating bonus of 9d per shift.

There is uncertainty about when women began to invade the masculine world of the Wakefield gas business. Undoubtedly the first were replacements for those who 'marched away for king and country' during the First World War. As they were paid substantially less than their male colleagues, management saw them as a means of reducing the wage bill. There is nothing to suggest that women employed on slot-meter duties emptied fewer meters than men.

With the end of hostilities, the trade union was seeking the termination of the employment of the ten women. It is not known whether it was compliance or natural wastage, but by February 1919 there were only six on the payroll.

In 1904 the manager achieved his long-held ambition of having a high-street showroom with facilities for demonstrating a range of uses for gas. A building in Marygate was leased from Mr Brook at an initial rent of £27 pa (Figure 7). Some two years later fifteen schools took part in a company-sponsored cookery and laundry competition. The winner of the silver shield mounted on an oak panel was St James School, Thornes.

There was the threat of competition in 1846 when those who were dissatisfied with the price and quality of gas, and being ignored by the directors, decided to promote the Wakefield New Gas Company (prospectus dated 22 October 1846) and to seek Parliamentary approval for subsequent operations. Some 1788 townspeople supported the petition, together with the Wakefield Street Commissioners, the Surveyors of the Highway for the divisions of Kirkgate and Westgate in Wakefield and for Alverthorpe, Thornes,

Figure 7. The Wakefield Gaslight Company's showroom in Marygate, pictured in 1937. *Wakefield Library Headquarters*

Stanley and Wrenthorpe. Objectors to the formation of the new company were the Wakefield Gas Light Company, the Wakefield Water Company, the owners of nine mills and businesses, 28 gas consumers and 239 townspeople; that of the Aire and Calder Navigation Company was withdrawn. The response of Chairman Statter and his board was to set in motion an amendment to their Act of Parliament; there were to be 116 objectors. Both petitions were presented to the parliamentary examining committee on 4 July 1847. This decided that, as a duopoly would be against the public interest, they would adjourn proceedings until 7 July to enable agreement to be reached as to which petition was to proceed. After intensive negotiations the petition of the existing company was redrafted and that of the new company was withdrawn.

The Act of Parliament that received Royal assent on 9 July 1847 was to result in fundamental changes. It introduced tests for purity, pressure and illuminating value of gas supplied. There was a limitation on the price of gas and on the company's dividends. The amount of capital that could be raised (after undistributed profits had been capitalised) was limited to £7,500, with powers to borrow up to a third of the issued capital.

Powers to raise capital was one of the most important clauses in the Act of Parliament: the size of the amount authorised was of prime importance as it had a direct bearing on the number of times that money which could otherwise have been spent on developing the business was required to finance returning to Parliament. Each new application to Parliament provided local government and the public with an opportunity to effect change.

It is impossible to determine who was the first in Wakefield to use a gas cooker. The proximity of the coal fields deterred any significant challenge to the traditional coal-fired kitchen range but by the 1870s the tide was beginning to turn.: there were to be tariffs for different types of use, each being metered and a charge being made for the meter. In 1884 shareholders were informed that:

the directors had taken in hand a new business, the letting out of gas cookers and stoves on hire, which they believed would bring a considerable quantity of 'grist to the mill' by increasing the consumption of gas. In the first month they had let out 51 cookers and eight stoves. Several of the gas cookers were in use in public bakeries. (Figure 8)

By the centenary year the number of cookers on hire had increased to 2,513; in addition there were 3,986 breakfast grillers and 14,498

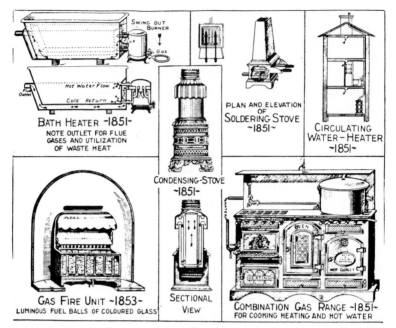

Figure 8. Gas appliances of the mid nineteenth century, compiled from various sources in the British Gas archives.

boiling rings. At the outbreak of the Second World War in 1939 there were 3,642 gas cookers, 5,580 gas fires, 648 gas water heaters and 31,862 other gas appliances (hair curlers, irons, pokers etc) on hire.

Generations of engineers and scientists had dreamed of the conversion of the latent energy of coal into an alternative to steam power; there are patents dating back to 1791. During the 1860s Ebenezer Goddard introduced a practical gas engine; however it was due to the efforts of a German engineer, Dr Otto, who in 1876 produced an engine using compression before combustion, with an economical cycle of operation, that the gas engine became a practical combustion engine.

The versatility of the gas engine was recognised from an early date in Wakefield, from driving lathes to grinding coffee beans at the grocer's. From the chairman's report for 1884 we learn:

there are 25 gas engines at work in the town, a considerable quantity of gas being used for other purposes than lighting.

The twentieth century heralded change, some the result of market forces, others company policy and nationalisation. For ten years of the first half of the century the country was engaged in world wars, and there was a decade of increasing national industrial unrest and deep trade depression.

At the outbreak of the Great War, in 1914, in addition to its traditional role of providing solid and gaseous fuel, the company was taking steps to meet government demands for the extraction of chemicals for strategic purposes. The benefits accruing extended far beyond the war years.

One of the non-technical problems resulting from the war was the shortage of coins for the slot meter. During the autumn of 1915 the master of the Royal Mint announced there would be no further issue of bronze coins, suggesting circulation would be improved by meters being emptied more frequently. Undoubtedly this considered wisdom was received at Wakefield as just another example of bureaucracy: with over 10,500 coin

> ## WHAT
> ## The Wakefield
> ## Gaslight Company
> ### DOES !
>
> 1. Keeps 120 Employees in Full-Time Employment.
> 2. Keeps 66 Miners Fully Employed.
> 3. Every Year Pays in Wages and Spends locally £45,000.
> 4. Subscribes to the local Rates over £4,000 per year.
> 5. Supplies one of the most Useful Commodities found in the Home, in the form of Gas, which is the essence of Coal and most economical to use.
> 6. Supplies the Best Smokeless Fuel in Sizes to suit its Customers.
> 7. Makes 35,000 gallons of Home Produced Motor Spirit annually
>
> MORAL. SUPPORT LOCAL INDUSTRY and if you have no Gas in your home, put it in and start saving TIME AND MONEY.

Figure 9. An advertisement by the Wakefield Gaslight Company in 1934 showing its civic consciousness and some sensitivity in regard to the coal industry.

meters and a depleted work force, management and the gas customer had a problem - until higher value coin mechanism became available.

The ending of hostilities should have heralded the return to peace time conditions; unfortunately the 1920s saw problems of supply and demand, with increased incidents of industrial unrest, placing unaccustomed responsibilities on management.

Post-war problems faced the directors including supplying gas to basically working-class customers during a period of industrial depression and the loss of customers, due to the demolition of property under slum-clearance schemes, exacerbated by the Wakefield Corporation policy of favouring electricity for their new estates. Further, there were problems of availability and the high price of the material required for renovation of the gas works (and district) which had of necessity been neglected during the war.

Figure 10. An advertisement by the Wakefield Gaslight Company in 1937.

The national coal strike (10 April - 4 July 1921) cost the company some £4,532 in maintaining the gas supply. The importation of foreign coal was locally a politically emotive subject. Notices appeared in the newspaper and on the cinema screen urging the conservation of gas (Figures 9 and 10).

In September 1935 the United Kingdom Gas Corporation sought unsuccessfully to negotiate the purchase of the Wakefield gas undertaking. In 1943, however, the terms they offered were received more favourably and acceptance was recommended. The transfer was effective from 1 January 1944 and at this point direction passed out of the hands of local people.

UKGC rationalised their West Yorkshire gas interests by the creation of the West Yorkshire group of companies - sixteen in all - with Wakefield as the administrative centre. To facilitate the movement of employees within the group, wages were standardised at the Morley level - a general upgrading.[12] Once again the company emerged from the war (1945) with the works and district showing signs of inadequate maintenance, and a climate that was not conducive to capital investment. 1945 came in like a lion: the period from 19 to 30 January was abnormally cold and it was necessary to seek the co-operation of industry in economising in the use of gas to maintain the domestic supply. It was early February before 'normal' operating was resumed. The coal situation in 1946 was bad, but worse in 1947; it was only through the skilful utilisation of scarce resources by Mr Whitehead, the works superintendent, that there was any gas at all.

On Sunday 1 May 1949 all the assets and liabilities of the company became vested in the North Eastern Gas Board.

The discovery of reserves of natural gas had a profound effect on the nationalised industry. No longer was it to be the captive customer of a rival fuel competitor and subject to the constant spiral of price increases. During the summer of 1966 the decision was taken to supply gas in its 'natural' state to customers. The decade 1967-1977

Figure 11. The redundant gasholder just off Jacob's Well Lane, 1999. Kate Taylor.

was to witness a unique industrial exercise as upwards of 40 million gas appliances of all descriptions, owned by 14 million customers, were identified and, where possible, modified to burn the new fuel from the North Sea, and later Morecambe bay. The work was carried out without any direct charge to the appliance owner. Gas conversion at Wakefield was effected between 6 October 1975 and 8 January 1976.[13]

During 1986 the gas business turned full circle with privatisation and the creation of British Gas Plc (Figure 11).

Notes and References

1. Walter T Layton, *The Discovery of Gas Lighting. Notes on the Life and Work of the Rev. John Clayton DD 1657-1725*, London 1927; A letter from John Clayton to the Royal Society, 12 May 1688, giving account of several observations, *Philosophical Transactions*, no 201, 1693, pp781-789.
2. *Wakefield Star*, 17 January 1806.
3. *Wakefield and Halifax Journal*, 3 April 1818
4. Henry Clarkson, *Memories of Merry Wakefield*, 1896.
5. *Wakefield and Halifax Journal*, August 1822.
6. Land Registry, West Yorkshire Archive Service, Wakefield.
7. K O M Golisti, *Gas Adventure - the Malam Influence*.
8. K O M Golisti, *Gas Adventure at Wakefield*.
9. *Wakefield and Halifax Journal*, 7 February 1823.
10. Evidence given to Parliamentary surveyors in 1846, British Gas Archives, Partington.
11. Minute of directors' meeting February 1902, Minute Book, British Gas Archives.
12. *Ibid.* September 1944.
13. British Gas Corporation Negas Region – Conversion Reports, British Gas Archives.

2. WAKEFIELD'S SIGNIFICANCE TO A WIDER WORLD

by John Goodchild

THE WAKEFIELD AREA, like many another in this country, has produced its 'firsts' in the sense of being the place where an idea or a structure or an institution was first thought of or implemented. Sometimes these 'firsts' were of purely local significance, sometimes of regional concern, and sometimes of national and even international significance. A few are reasonably well known, but many are completely unrecognised and yet themselves also of international significance. In many cases a structure survives to illustrate the physical form of the innovation, although frequently somewhat altered in its character; in many instances insufficient is known about the world situation to enable other than a possible or probable tag to be attached to it as a first. In almost all cases these sometimes world firsts here are outside the rudimentary tourist strategy of the local authority. It is hoped that the publication of this essay will both bring this list of Wakefield area's firsts to the attention of the public and bring further information and comment forward. In almost every instance mentioned here, illustrative documentation on the matter is contained in John Goodchild's Local History Study Centre at Wakefield, and it is upon that information, coupled with background reading on each specific subject, that the content of this essay is based.

Probably the Wakefield area's most significant contribution to the world's development was the opening in 1798 of the Lake Lock Rail Road, running from above Outwood to the boats in the River Calder at Lake Lock below (the later) Stanley Church (Figure 1). This was not, of course, the world's first railway, or even the first in this area, but it may be claimed as the railway which introduced to the world the idea of both a railway company and a public railway (for the use of which a payment was made), twin and

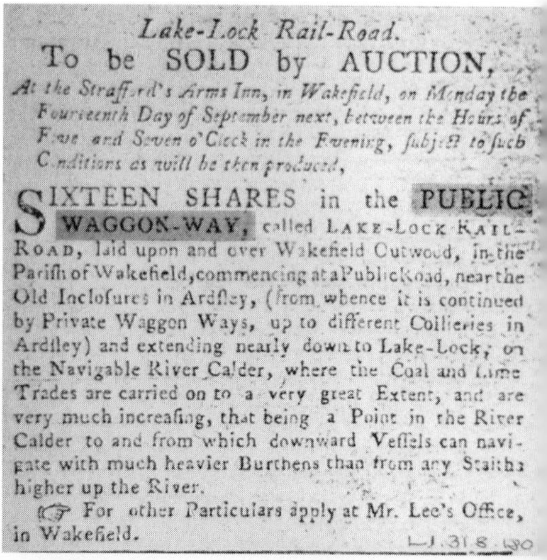

Figure 1. An advertisement of 1801 for shares in the Lake Lock rail-road. *The John Goodchild Collection*

Lake-Lock Rail-Road.
To be SOLD by AUCTION,
At the Strafford's Arms Inn, in Wakefield, on Monday the Fourteenth Day of September next, between the Hours of Five and Seven o'Clock in the Evening, subject to such Conditions as will be then produced,

SIXTEEN SHARES in the PUBLIC WAGGON-WAY, called LAKE-LOCK RAIL-ROAD, laid upon and over Wakefield Outwood, in the Parish of Wakefield, commencing at a Public Road, near the Old Inclosures in Ardsley, (from whence it is continued by Private Waggon Ways, up to different Collieries in Ardsley) and extending nearly down to Lake-Lock, on the Navigable River Calder, where the Coal and Lime Trades are carried on to a very great Extent, and are very much increasing, that being a Point in the River Calder to and from which downward Vessels can navigate with much heavier Burthens than from any Staiths higher up the River.

☞ For other Particulars apply at Mr. Lee's Office, in Wakefield.

associated ideas which were to cause the spread of railway networks throughout the whole world. The line itself was horse hauled, with (early) iron edge rails, and largely coal carrying, in which it was not unusual; what was unusual was its basic principle of utilising the capital of a number of individual shareholders to form a railway company which then constructed the line and maintained it, allowing public use (with the charging of a toll for that use) to provide the company's income. The line closed in 1836 and the company's existence was wound up finally in the mid-1850s, but considerable remains of the railway are still to be seen on the ground between Bottomboat and Carr Gate.

One of the men behind the Lake Lock Rail Company's project was the Wakefield lawyer and speculator, John Lee (1759-1836), the subject of the present writer's book, *Attorney at Large* (Wakefield, 1986). Lee was also a committee member of the Barnsley Canal Company, formed in 1793 to build a canal – the eighteenth century equivalent of a modern motorway – between Wakefield, Barnsley and Silkstone. The construction of this canal began in 1793, and it passed over the watershed between the valleys of the Calder and Dearne rivers, a route involving the construction of two great rock cuttings, one at Walton and the larger at Notton. The latter was of

necessity very deep and may well have been the greatest hole in the earth to that time constructed in England; at the other great cutting, that at Walton, stone-built barracks for the workmen or navvies were built and have survived – perhaps the only such eighteenth century workmen's accommodation so to do. Both of the cuttings remain and can be walked through on the towpath; the navvies' accommodation exists in the form of the house above the cutting lip at Walton, still known as Stone Heaps. The Barnsley Canal itself awaits local authority support for its reopening, although it has an enthusiastic and active Barnsley Canal Society.

John Lee the lawyer and

Figure 2. The terrace on the north side of St John's Square.

Figure 3. Stanley Ferry Aqueduct, 1999. *Kate Taylor*

entrepreneur was also responsible for the building – indeed for the whole idea – of the St John's development on the outskirts of Wakefield: the New Town of Wakefield as he knew it (Figure 2). Georgian housing developments for the residence of the well-to-do were of course common in the eighteenth century, but this near Wakefield was unusual – perhaps unique – in that it lay not contiguous to the old town, but at a half a mile's distance from it: some half mile of then open countryside lay between old Wakefield, extending then only as far as its medieval limit, where now the Court House stands in Wood Street, and the new town, now called St John's, on its healthy hilltop site to the north. This new town was built to be open to the sun from the south: what is now known as St John's Square was in fact only two sides of a square and was known as St John's Place (using the name of the new church which was built as its centrepiece and consecrated in 1795), and St John's Street (now St John's North) also had no houses on its southern side. The whole scheme was built to a uniform frontage elevation (but not so the backs of the development) and was built between 1791 and c1803. Another apparent English first.

The great cast and wrought iron aqueduct across the River Calder at Stanley Ferry has been said to be perhaps England's least well known canal structure of major significance (Figure 3). It was opened in 1839 with the passage across it of a Wakefield-built seagoing schooner, and the aqueduct itself carried the new, direct line of the Aire and Calder Navigation's Wakefield waterway line,

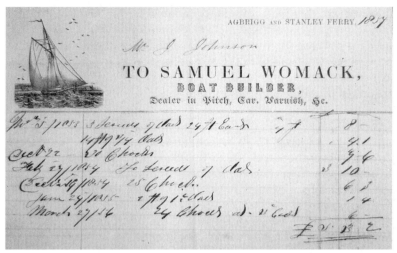

Figure 4. An invoice of 1857 from the boat builder, Samuel Womack.
The John Goodchild Collection

built under its *Act of 1828*. The aqueduct is now a scheduled ancient monument, and is adjoined by British Waterway's Stanley Ferry Yard, an early example of prefabricated building still very actively in use and where the use of the dry docks and modern lock-gate building can still be witnessed.

The schooner James, which was used to inaugurate the aqueduct, was built at Wakefield, one among several such vessels which were intended purely for sea work and which would never return to Wakefield. The town and its environs had several boat and ship building yards and was perhaps the most inland location in Britain at which seagoing ships were regularly built.

The remains of one of these yards is very visible at the bottom of Heath Common, on the line of the Barnsley Canal, and has the added unusual interest of account books from its work surviving today (Figure 4).

Wakefield was, of course, an important inland port, the meeting place of three major and successful waterway routes (one of them leading to trans-Pennine waterways) and especially concerned with large trades in the downstream carriage of coal and the upstream trade in corn and raw wool, although many other commodities were also carried.

At Ossett, there was founded in 1785 what may have been England's first co-operative manufacturing mill: the Ossett Mill Company's Ossett Mill (now Healey Old Mill) at Healey. This was financed by the joint capital of a number of operative master handloom weavers and Wakefield cloth merchants, to provide a much needed, powered (by waterwheels on a goit from the Calder) mill to process raw wool and to full (felt) woollen cloths. It can be envisaged as perhaps the first example of such co-operation in manufacturing by power in the country; a few remains of the old mill can still be seen.

Two Wakefield roads can lay claim to being of more than regional interest: the earlier is the Wakefield and Aberford road – a new and direct route to the Great North Road going north, and a new route to York – which was again promoted by John Lee, who owned an extensive estate at Stanley on its route. It was perhaps the region's first new highway: it linked up (by major sections of new road) parts of older routes, to give a direct way to the north and York, and was built under the powers of an Act obtained in 1789. The Ings Road was, like the Aberford road, a turnpike or toll road, and again had John Lee behind it, who owned land in Wakefield Ings. Built in the early 1830s, it was intended to both open up land in the Ings and provide a bypass to Wakefield with its central, narrow and congested streets, but its possession of a tollbar (at the crossing with the also new Denby Dale Road) was a deterrent to its use by through traffic, and it was not until it was freed from toll by its purchase by Wakefield Corporation in the 1860s, that it became increasingly the boon to traffic which it very much is today. It was also one of England's shortest independent turnpike roads.

A much more well known Wakefield first was Charles ('Squire') Waterton's considered creation of the world's first nature sanctuary in the form of his park around Walton Hall. Waterton (1782–1865) erected a substantial (though cheaply-built) wall around his park,

Figure 5. The Barnsley Canal and the wall round Squire Waterton's grounds at Walton. *The John Goodchild Collection.*

with a higher section where it was near the Barnsley Canal, since boatmen were regarded as likely poachers, and he encouraged the development there of a sanctuary for birds and animals, while allowing pre-booked parties of visitors to enjoy the extraordinary scenery – where else is there a mansion set in an island in a lake between wooded hills? – and the use of his (now much decayed but still recognisable) grotto area for their picnics and games (Figure 5). He was himself to be buried within the area of his own nature sanctuary; much of the area is now, inappropriately, a private golfcourse.

Below Westgate Chapel in Wakefield are catacombs for the interment of the dead, and there are buried some sixty of the principal inhabitants of Wakefield and its vicinity of the late eighteenth and nineteenth centuries, including several ex MPs, several cloth merchant princes, a provincial grand master of the Freemasons, etc (Figure 6). The catacombs were planned (except for an extension to them made early in the nineteenth century) as part of the Chapel structure, which was opened in 1752, but which, incidentally, includes much woodwork from an earlier chapel of 1697. The catacombs seem to be the earliest known in England as public catacombs, ie where anyone rather than a particular family, could be interred; they were to be followed in and about Wakefield

Figure 6. Westgate Chapel catacombs.

by catacombs built under the new churches of St John's, Alverthorpe, and Stanley, but to a different scheme. Parts of the St John's catacombs also survive today.

It is curious how individuals connect together some of these Wakefield area firsts: John Lee has been mentioned, but Benjamin Heywood (for whose home the present Stanley Hall was built) was chairman of the Lake Lock Rail Road Company for many years and a committee member of the Ossett Mill Company, and he is buried in the catacombs of Westgate Chapel, while he was also concerned with the new Aberford turnpike road. Charles Waterton's father had been a committee man of the Barnsley Canal Company, and indeed the natural route for the canal would have been through his park rather than through the Walton cutting, although of course the park was avoided. A monument in Westgate Chapel commemorated Henry Briggs (1797–1868), the chairman of that congregation, a member of the family colliery partnership at Flockton and Shitlington which ran the model social system in connection with their collieries to which the Commissioners investigating the employment of women and children in mines in 1841 devoted so much space, and which included the provision of such otherwise unheard–of facilities as a theatre (plays and musical events), a running track, a discussion group between masters and men, a sports ground, and so forth. Later, opening his own collieries at Whitwood near Normanton from 1839. Henry Briggs introduced with his sons in 1865 the idea of profit-sharing with his workmen – an innovation which caused international interest – and after his death, in 1869, a worker-director on the Board of his company was introduced too.

Henry Briggs was an active Liberal in his politics, in a period when Wakefield attracted national attention (at least) on account of its deserved reputation as the most consistently corrupt Parliamentary borough in this country. Wakefield had been enfranchised only in 1832, when Daniel Gaskell of Lupset Hall was returned, unopposed (solely because the Tories had not got their act together) in the radical liberal interest. By the 1850s, however, bribery, corruption and even intimidation had set in; some Parliamentary candidates here were mere carpet-baggers, but it was in 1859 that the worst (reported) excesses occurred, one of the (ultimately unusual) Parliamentary Inquiries resulting in the imprisonment and fining of some Tories and the usual evidence being forthcoming at one Inquiry from old ladies who 'happened' to have been looking through their curtains and seen bribes being offered. In regard to at least the curtain-twitching, nothing changes! The election of 1880 was the last when the unsuccessful political party (the Tories as it happened) thought of raising the question after the election, but then thought better of it. From 1859 the right to return a Member had been refused to Wakefield for over two years, as a punishment for consistent corruption, and even the (Tory) *Times* newspaper had castigated the electors and non-electors of the Borough of Wakefield for their bribery; elections were certainly jolly affairs in those days.

One might mention a whole range of other Wakefield firsts: a few, very briefly described, are as follows. The colliery railway tunnel under New Hall Approach, Shitlington, is of c1790 and is perhaps the oldest railway tunnel in the world remaining open: the twenty-arch viaduct beyond it was in existence by 1803 (Figure 7). Both were built for the colliery owner, James Milnes. The use of gas as an illuminant was first brought to public attention by a rector of Crofton in the seventeenth century. Sharlston Hall has a porch and entrance, with an inscription, built by a sixteenth-century colliery owner, and the extensive remains of shallow-shaft mines remain near by on Sharlston Common, while New Sharlston colliery village, of the late 1860s and 1870s, with its chapel, school, Co-op store and of course its houses, remains intact (although tarted).

Wakefield had a unique system of chantry chapels at the four main road entrances to the town, most of them being founded through the giving of the inhabitants rather than being the gift of some great man; so too the great medieval church (from 1888 the cathedral) mirrors the charitable piety of the inhabitants, with its tower and spire the highest in Yorkshire at 247 feet (Figure 8). Lollardy – incipient Protestantism – is recorded in Wakefield long before the

Figure 7. Flockton railway viaduct. *The John Goodchild Collection.*

Reformation and Wakefield the first community in Yorkshire reported to possess it. Parliamentarian support, movements for Parliamentary reform, Chartism, radicalism, Christian Socialism, were all strongly and early supported here. The town became a self-governing borough (by purchase of that right) in c1190, before Leeds and other local towns; it never possessed a town wall. Here were printed (by William Nicholson) among the first British cheap books, at his works in Vicarage Street; here was trained Titus Salt in the raw wool trade – who went on to become one of the great Victorian industrialists and paternalist capitalists. Here too was trained William Whiteley, the developer of the great multi-department Victorian store, Whiteley's, in London; here James Aspdin produced the first Portland cement – and the *Wakefield Arms* may be an early example of a surviving building using that material (Figure 9). Here, at Lower Altofts, were model colliers' houses which included what was claimed to be the

Figure 8. The spire of Wakefield Cathedral, taken about 1880 when it was Wakefield's parish church.

Figure 9. The Wakefield Arms. *Kate Taylor.*

longest three-storey row in Europe; here were invented Tom Puddings, the iron (later steel) compartment boats which travelled in a train of up to nineteen, carrying mainly coal to the docks at Goole; here the banking firm of Leatham, Tew & Co (whose building, with their initials on it, survives as Barclay's bank in Wood Street) were among the last to issue their own private banknotes. The area possessed what was probably the authorised railway company with the longest title of any – the Sheffield, Rotherham, Barnsley, Wakefield, Huddersfield and Goole company – and Wakefield's so-called 99 arches spanning the Calder valley (there are some 95 arches in fact) is one of the longest. It was opened in two sections, in 1857 and 1866. Here (again at Altofts) Sir William Garforth proved the influence of coal dust in colliery underground explosions; here was brought up George Gissing (1857–1903), the Victorian novelist whose works have gained some international reputation; here have been born many other famous men and women, although they have nearly all had the sense to clear out of Wakefield as soon as possible: in our own day, David Storey (b1933) the novelist and Barbara Hepworth (1903–1975) the sculptress, among others.

These are only some of Wakefield's contributions to society in, but also far beyond, the local area. There are of course others.

3. OSSETT AND THE GREAT WAR

by David Scriven

WHEN SHE LEFT OSSETT Miss Annie Sharp was no doubt looking forward to her tour of Belgium. By Monday 3 August 1914 she had reached Dinant in the south-east of the country. On the same day German cavalry passed through the town. Miss Sharp and her party fled. The trains were crowded, the cross-channel ferry was equally full, but on Tuesday 4 August she was safe in London. At 11.00pm on that day Britain went to war against Germany in defence of Belgian neutrality.

While Annie Sharp was fleeing from Belgium, the Ossett members of the Territorial Army were on their way back to the town from their camp at Whitby. On Wednesday evening, following the arrival of their mobilisation papers, 83 members of the detachment marched from their Drill Hall in Station Road to their billet at the Town Hall in Wakefield. A large crowd gathered to give the men a 'hearty' send off and local tradesmen showed their support by giving the men sandwiches, tobacco and cigarettes.

Later that evening the ringing of the Ossett Town Hall bells attracted several hundred people to the Market Place where they heard the mayor, Councillor H Robinson, read eleven royal proclamations from the town hall steps. At the end of the twenty-minute reading the crowd responded with gusto to the mayor's request for the singing of *God Save the King*.

Wednesday was the first day that the shops were open after the August Bank Holiday. Fear of food shortages led to panic buying and prices rose sharply with flour increasing from 1s 6d (7.5p) to 3s (15p) a stone. A special meeting of the Ossett and Horbury Trades and Labour Council condemned the increase as unpatriotic while the *Ossett Observer* accused hoarders of creating problems for the future. However, official assurances in the daily newspapers that food supplies were sufficient for several months had a calming effect. By the end of the week prices had fallen with the cost of flour dropping to 2s (10p) a stone.

The outlook for the town's staple industry, reclaimed wool, was poor in the first days of the conflict. War cut off continental supplies of rags and led to the cancellation of orders for reclaimed wool.

Figure 1. A newly mobilised contingent of Ossett's Territorial Army detachment left their drill hall in Station Road on the evening of 5 August 1914 witnessed by a large crowd of wellwishers. Later in the war the hall was used by the Volunteer Training Corps, a home defence force. *David Scriven*

Faced by a rise in unemployment, the mayor called a meeting of employers to consider ways of minimising hardship. The difficulties of Ossett's businessmen were compounded by the closure of banks until Friday. When they reopened the Ossett banks had enough gold and silver coinage to meet local needs, but none of the new £1 and 10s notes. However the Post Office reminded its customers that postal orders could be used as currency during the financial difficulties.

During the hectic days following the outbreak of war, no one in Ossett could accurately predict how the town would be affected by the conflict. This essay attempts to show how life in this small Yorkshire town was changed by war's demands.

Until 1916 the government depended on volunteers to fill the ranks of the armed forces. In Ossett the local territorial detachment, part of the 4th Battalion of the KOYLI, was mobilised in the first week of the war (Figure 1). The territorials were only committed to home duties but by the beginning of September the entire Ossett detachment had volunteered for overseas service. While the territorials were being mobilised, the army and navy reservists living in the town also received their call-up papers. Before the war there had been some criticism of the territorials and the reservists. The *Ossett Observer* now commented that the 'cheap sneers' directed at them had now a 'sharply pointed reply'.[1]

A national recruiting campaign to raise volunteers for Kitchener's New Army began in August 1914. In Ossett the mayor, Councillor H Robinson, started the local campaign with an article in the *Ossett Observer*. His opening words stressed how serious the situation was:

We must not merely fight - we must win, or as a nation go under.[2]

Appealing for men to enlist, he called upon employers to keep open the jobs of volunteers and to top up their army wages so their families did not suffer hardship. As an example to others, he wrote, the Borough Council would make weekly payments to any of its employees who volunteered. For single men these would be 7s 6d (37.5p) and for married men 12s 6d (62.5p) with 2s 6d (12.5p) extra for each child.

The mayor's appeal was followed during the next year by meetings, rallies and newspaper advertisements publicising the need for volunteers. Men who had enlisted put additional moral pressure on those reluctant to join up by expressing their contempt for 'shirkers'. This stage of the campaign culminated in August 1915 when a detachment of the 11th KOYLI held manoeuvres in Gedham Field and there were recruiting meetings at works throughout Ossett.

The aim of this campaign was to raise two platoons, 128 men, in Ossett and Horbury, but the results were disappointing. Nevertheless, the *Ossett Observer* believed that over the year the town had contributed its fair share to Kitchener's New Army. This illusion was dispelled when it used official figures to calculate that only 500 men in Ossett had joined up, a figure far below the 630 it thought should have enlisted. The *Observer* did not give an explanation for the disappointing figure but it seems likely that the boom in the woollen and reclaimed wool industries deterred men from enlisting because work was so plentiful.

Conscription was the solution eventually adopted to the problem of recruitment. The compilation of a National Register in 1915 gave the government a picture of the country's manpower resources. In Ossett the work of drawing up the local register was carried out by the Borough Council in August and September. It showed that in the town there were 2,000 men of military age, 600 of them starred as men vital to the industrial effort and 1,400 of the unstarred. However, before the National Register was used to conscript men, one last effort was made to save voluntary enlistment - the Derby scheme.

Under this men 'attested' their readiness to serve when called upon. To publicise it eligible men were sent a letter from Lord Derby inviting them to attest. In Ossett the postal authorities delivered in November 1915 almost 1,400 of the letters. To back up these it was planned to carry out a canvass of all eligible men in the town. Unfortunately the local committee in charge of the canvass did not have enough volunteers to carry it out. Instead it invited men to attest at the Town Hall. At first there was some confusion about the position of starred men, but Major Smith, the area's chief recruiting officer, made it clear that they should attest as well as unstarred men. As a result, Alderman Robinson and Edmund Lund visited all the farms, munition works and collieries in Ossett and Horbury to make sure that starred men did attest. In January 1916 the *Ossett Observer* concluded that the Derby scheme had been a success in the town: 64 per cent of single men and 66 per cent of married men eligible for the scheme had enlisted, attested or had offered to do so but had been rejected on medical grounds.

Nationally, however, the Derby scheme was judged a failure and conscription was therefore introduced in January 1916 by the *Military Service Act*. Conscription had been discussed by the Chamber of Commerce and the Trades and Labour Council in the previous year. Neither body had seen the need for compulsion then, but once it was introduced neither opposed it. However there was suspicion among some workers in the town that the real purpose of conscription was to lower soldiers' wages and to bring industry under military control. The increasing power of the military certainly worried the Trades and Labour Council and also some Liberals. J A Rushby, secretary of the Liberal Club, said in January 1916 that

> *unless they guarded their rights there was a danger of militarism being fostered in England.*[3]

Under the Derby scheme local appeal tribunals were appointed so that men could ask for a postponement of service. These continued in existence once conscription was introduced and now dealt not only with appeals for deferral but also conscientious objections to the war. Ossett's tribunal was headed by the mayor, Alderman G F Wilson, and included five other members of the corporation together with a representative each from the Chamber of Commerce and the Trades and Labour Council. When the tribunal began its work in February 1916, the *Ossett Observer* was struck by the informality of its proceedings and the 'courteous manner' in which each claimant was dealt with.[4] Most of the cases appearing before the tribunal were for exemption from military service on grounds other than those of conscience. It was possible to argue, for example, that a man's contribution to a business was so important that he could not be spared. This was the case put by the mayor himself when, following a raising of the age of military service and his resignation from the tribunal, he appeared before it in June 1918. Alderman Wilson explained that his claim was on business grounds. He had sole responsibility for a reclaimed wool firm with a turnover of £100,000 and 95 employees. If he were called up he would have to close the business. The tribunal was sympathetic and granted him exemption from military service for six months.

By the beginning of April 1916, 267 applications for exemption had been reviewed by the tribunal. Of these only six were on conscientious grounds. The arguments used by the objector were religious and moral but they failed to impress the tribunal; all were refused. One objector was, however, directed to non-combatant service, a decision he accepted. The few conscientious objectors who came before the tribunal after March 1916 also had their applications rejected. Of these only one, eighteen-year old Roland Smith, carried his opposition to bloodshed as far as ignoring his calling-up papers. Fined 40s (£2) by the borough court, and remanded to wait for a military escort, he declared that he would not pay his fine.

Local tribunals such as Ossett's were under constant pressure to minimise exemptions. In both 1917 and 1918 the military instructed the Ossett tribunal to review the conditional exemptions it had granted and there seems to have been an increasing number of appeals against its decisions by the national service representative. These were likely to be granted as the chairman of the West Riding Appeal Tribunal referred more than once to the leniency of the Ossett tribunal.

By the beginning of 1918 Ossett had sent between 1,350 and 1,500 men to the armed forces. For the families of these men, separation from sons and husbands could lead to considerable mental distress and one Ossett father was driven to suicide by worry about his son who had been in France for fifteen months. Letters and postcards to some extent eased the pain of separation and extracts from soldiers' letters were frequently printed in the local papers. This encouraged Mrs Hanson of the Gables, Station Road, to forward her son's letter to the *Wakefield Express*. Lieutenant Hanson wrote:

I really believe more in fate each show I am in. I still have wonderful luck. I got a very slight hit on the cheek but nothing much and I have discovered a bullet in the heel of my boot.[5]

Much more welcome than letters, and much rarer, were leave visits. These were so valued that teachers, and no doubt other workers as well, took time off when family members came home on leave. At Holy Trinity Infants School, for example, Mrs Nettleton was absent in March 1917 when her husband had his last leave before being posted abroad.[6]

One solder who created a mild sensation while on leave in 1914 was private Sidney Cecil Beauchamp whose stories of his part in the Battle of the Marne were reported in the *Ossett Observer*. However it was soon revealed that although Beauchamp had enlisted, he had been discharged on medical grounds and had never been to France. Furthermore, he not only had a wife in Ossett but two others elsewhere in the country. Arrested in Hull, he was tried at Glamorgan Assizes in March 1915 and sentenced to three years' imprisonment for bigamy.

Miss Bedford has been absent since Tuesday morning owing to the death of her brother, who was killed in action.[7]

The War Office telegram bringing news of a soldier's death was a devastating blow for a family. Of the Ossett men who served in the armed forces, 230 died during the war. Their brief lives were commemorated in the local press by obituaries, usually accompanied by photographs of the men in uniform. Grieving was made difficult because those who died abroad were buried there. Some consolation might be sought, however, in a memorial service such as that held for Private W Ward in Zion Congregational Chapel, Gawthorpe, in August 1917.

By then some in Ossett were beginning to feel that the town's dead needed a permanent memorial. In October of that year, the mayor, Alderman G F Wilson, called a public meeting to discuss the matter. Although attendance was small, a committee was formed to consider proposals. Among the suggestions for a memorial were a park for each of the borough's wards, an endowment for Dewsbury Infirmary and scholarships for the sons and daughters of soldiers. One particularly striking proposal was for the creation of a lake behind Spa Street School. At the centre of the lake there was to be an island with a bronze statue of Britannia rescuing her child from an eagle. Not all of the ideas met with approval. Thomas Westwood opposed a YMCA social club since it would attract young lads away from the town's Sunday Schools. With so many suggestions to consider, the committee decided to consult Ossett's servicemen when their Christmas gifts were sent to them.

Figure 2. Ossett's war memorial was dedicated on 11 November 1928 by Viscount Lascelles. It commemorated the 230 Ossett men who died in the Great War. *David Scriven.*

After initial interest in the memorial scheme there was a long period when no progress was made. Not until November 1918 did the committee submit to a public meeting four schemes for consideration. These were for a permanent roll of honour, recreation grounds for children, a fund to relieve war widows of rent and rates, and public baths. No decision was reached because attendance at the meeting was so small - an insult to the soldiers was one description - that it was adjourned for two months. Given such lack of public interest, it is not surprising that it was not until 1928 that a war memorial scheme was carried out (Figure 2).

With the regular army and the territorials in France in the autumn of 1914, the country seemed to be vulnerable to a German invasion. To counter this threat volunteer forces began to be formed. An Ossett and Horbury force was created in October 1915 with James Fitton as its president. Although the unit only took men ineligible for military service, it had a membership of 170 by the beginning of 1915. The members drilled three times weekly and improved their marksmanship on three miniature rifle ranges, including one at the drill hall in Station Road.

During 1915 the volunteers continued to recruit. The sinking of the *Lusitania* was followed by an advertisement in the *Ossett Observer*:

AN APPEAL. LUSITANIA VICTIMS CRY TO YOU
SHOULD THE GERMANS COME!
Are you prepared?
Could you protect - may be avenge - the women and children?
Are you trained?
Can you shoot?
IF NOT, WHY NOT?[8]

The volunteers' facilities improved with the provision of an open-air rifle range in Horbury, while their appearance perhaps became more military when they decided that members could buy uniforms at £2 each. This decision was prompted by the affiliation of the Ossett and Horbury volunteers to the Wakefield Battalion of the Volunteer Training Corps.

With the introduction of the Derby scheme, the local volunteers offered to organise drilling for men who enlisted and wanted preliminary training before being called up. When the twice weekly drills started in January 1916 at the territorial hall in Station Road, the first was attended by 68 men. The Ossett appeal tribunal made training with the volunteers one of the conditions for some of the exemptions from military service. Enough men ignored this condition for the volunteers' officers to complain that the tribunal was not enforcing it strictly enough. On the other hand, there were protests from the men at the abusive language of the army officers who carried out the drills.

The German army did not land in Britain, but Zeppelins did bomb British towns. The Zeppelin threat led to a brief imposition of lighting restrictions in Ossett in 1915 when alternate street lamps were left unlit. More severe restrictions were imposed on the town at the beginning of 1916. All outside lamps had to be extinguished, except those needed for safety, the lighting of shop fronts had to be dimmed and all interiors had to be blacked out. There was criticism in Ossett of the severity of these restrictions, particularly as they did not apply at first to the nearby town of Horbury. Councillor Stead feared that they

> *would have a depressing effect on the public generally and especially on the feebler sex.*[9]

Such complaints had no influence and there was a rush to buy blinds. Some churches, such as St Ignatius, found it impossible to black out their windows and decided to hold services on Sunday afternoons rather than on Sunday evenings. To help pedestrians on the dark streets, the town council had the kerbs of the street corners whitened and each lamp post was painted with a white band.

Not all Ossett took the lighting restrictions seriously, leading to a complaint from a special constable in May 1916 that there were too many lights showing in the town. The special constables helped to enforce the restrictions and the borough court fined offenders who failed to observe the blackout. Thus, in October 1916 the landlord of the *Beehive Inn* in Gawthorpe was fined 13s (65p) for showing lights. In the following month the licensee of the *Masons' Arms* was fined 9s (45p) for a similar offence.

The risk of Zeppelin attacks led the council to publish advice about behaviour during air raids. An advertisement in the *Ossett Observer* in May 1915 urged people not to gather in the streets but to seek shelter in cellars or lower rooms. Unexploded bombs were not to be touched but were to be reported to the police. In February 1916 another newspaper advertisement informed the public that the warning for an air raid would be a reduction in gas pressure leading to a dimming of lights. The precautions were tested three times in 1916 and once in 1918 when the town was put on alert. Fortunately none of the warnings was followed by a raid.

The war not only brought the threat of aerial attacks but also led to an exaggerated fear of German espionage activities in Britain. One early victim of this alarm was Alex la Touche, son of a local doctor, whose wireless telegraph was put out of action as part of precautions against the interception of wireless messages. Such measures possibly heightened worries about German spies. J S Sanderson wrote to the *Ossett Observer* in October 1914 to draw attention to the strange flashes he had seen in the sky on two nights. 'Are they pre-arranged signals of the German Secret Service Corps?' he inquired.[10]

Alarm about German spies helped to stimulate hostility towards people of German and Austrian descent living in Britain. When the war began there were apparently no such families in the town, but in September 1914 a correspondent in the *Ossett Observer* defended the Andrassy family of Horbury against the 'lies' being spread about them. Fear of enemy aliens led the government to introduce internment for unnaturalised male Germans, Austrians and Hungarians of military age. One internment camp was opened at Lofthouse Park[11] and in 1917 the wife of one of the internees came to lodge with Mrs Laura Hart in Manor Road. Mrs Hart's failure to register her lodger with the police led to her appearance before local magistrates, but the case was dismissed with the magistrates generously paying the costs themselves. As the war continued there were demands for harsher measures against enemy aliens. At a public meeting in Ossett in July 1918 there were calls for the internment of all classes of 'enemy blood' and the removal from public office of all people of 'enemy blood', naturalised or not. Supporting these demands, Alderman H Robinson argued that every German at large was a potential danger, even if he were supporting Britain, as his national instinct might awaken at any moment. It was to appease such feelings that in the following month the government took powers to revoke the citizenship of naturalised Germans and Austrians.

The war had a major impact on the world of work in Ossett. After the initial difficulties the reclaimed wool industry entered a boom which lasted until the war's end. This was because although reclaimed wool was not used to any great extent in army uniforms, it was used in heavy overcoatings and blankets, and there was a huge demand for these. The boom was reflected in a steep rise in the cost of rags: by the end of 1916 prices were three to four times as high as they had been in 1914. These higher prices led to more rags being collected in Britain and this to some extent compensated for the reduction in continental supplies. In addition, the enlistment of millions of men resulted in more discarded clothes entering the market.

Nevertheless firms in the reclaiming industry did face problems in meeting demand. A labour shortage developed as men enlisted and as higher wages attracted men to other trades. This shortage was particularly felt in carbonising departments because of the unpleasant nature of their work. A further problem was shortage of dyes. Before the war most artificial dyes used in Britain had been made in Germany. With the outbreak of war this source was cut off and until alternative sources could be found dyestuffs were scarce and expensive.

At first the army sold its own discarded clothing to private industry for conversion into reclaimed wool and then bought back goods made from the wool. In 1916 it decided to cut its costs by processing its own waste clothing, and depots were set up in Dewsbury and Ossett. At the latter, at Northfield Mill in Church Street, 40-50 men and women were employed in sorting and repairing clothing (Figure 3). Garments beyond repair were sent to manufacturers doing government work. The scheme owed much to William E Gundill of Henry Cullingworth and Sons, rag merchants, who was awarded an OBE in 1918 in recognition of his work.

The town's coal mines had to meet an increased demand, partly because of the boom in the local wool and reclaimed wool

Figure 3. Northfield Mill in Church Street was used from 1916 as a military depot for recycling army clothing. *David Scriven.*

industries. Perhaps in response, the Low Laithes Colliery in Gawthorpe developed the Beeston seam in 1915. Eventually, however, the local pits faced severe problems in meeting demand as miners enlisted, and there was a shortage of railway trucks at Low Laithes and Roundwood Collieries. Output declined in the last years of the war and in 1918 it was 60 per cent of the pre-war level.

Although the town's engineering firms were small and few in number, they too made a contribution to the war effort. In April 1915 three of these firms, J Halstead and Son, J Redgewick and Sons, and Moses and Naylor, were represented at a meeting in Wakefield which considered a shell-making scheme. A committee was appointed to draw up plans, but in the following month Mr Halstead complained that the scheme had 'fizzled out' because of lack of official interest. Yet soon afterwards Ossett engineering firms did begin to receive orders for shell parts. Another local firm in receipt of government orders was Riley and Sons, firework makers, whose works were filling 75,000 hand grenades a week by September 1915. Some of the raw materials for explosives were made in Ossett. The town's gas works at Healey were equipped with a plant costing £550 to extract toluol and benzol, while at Victoria Mills the newly formed firm of Burrows (Chemicals) Limited began to make picric acid. Fumes from Victoria Mills soon provoked numerous complaints from nearby residents.

Ossett's farmers came under pressure in the last two years of the war to increase the amount of arable land on their farms to help meet the demand for cereals. Representatives from Ossett, East Ardsley and West Ardsley farmers formed a local Agricultural Advisory Committee in June 1917 to encourage grain growing. However, when members of the committee visited Ossett farmers they found some were reluctant to co-operate and they had to be reminded that they could be compelled to alter their cropping. As an incentive to plough more land, farmers were promised that tractors would be available at a charge of 15s an acre and that loans, repayable after the harvest, could be taken out to cover the costs.

Not only the country's farmers found the state increasingly intervening in their activities. Government intervention in the economy reached unprecedented levels during the war. The railways and coal mines were brought under state control; prices and profits in some industries were limited and the rationing of coal and foodstuffs was introduced. With so much regulation, it was easy to break rules. The engineering firm Spencer and Halstead was fined in 1917 for making mill repairs without official permission, while in the next year the Low Laithes Colliery Company was fined for letting railway wagons without official sanction.

One change introduced by the government to help industry in 1916 was British Summer Time. After the first summer under the new regime, the Chamber of Commerce pronounced it a great success. There had, for example, been great savings in gas and coal. However Ossett's farmers complained that they lost an extra hour in the morning during the harvest because dew made it impossible to work and then they had to pay for an hour's overtime at night. There were also complaints that children were out too late playing with the result that they were tired next day at school.

The wartime shortage of male labour was reflected in Ossett where the reclaimed wool, woollen and coal industries all had difficulties finding workers. One solution to the problem was to employ more women, but in Ossett the textile trades already depended heavily on female labour. In May 1915 one businessman noted that women workers were so scarce in Ossett that in future they would have to recruit women who had never done paid work. In spite of this, women did begin to fill new roles in the town. Female tram conductors, postal workers, and gas-meter readers made their appearance while Moses and Naylor employed munitionettes at their engineering works. In 1917 the local cinema, the Palladium, advertised for a 'Young lady to learn cinema operating'.[12]

This change in the composition of the labour force did not meet with resistance from the Trades and Labour Council but it wanted to ensure that women doing the same work as men were paid the same wages. This demand probably arose from the fear that in the post-war world cheap female labour might be used to undercut men's wages. Certainly when the council encouraged women workers to join trades unions it was so that 'probable capitalist pressure' at the end of the war could be resisted.

Labour relations in the town appear to have been good during the war. One possible source of friction was the rise in prices, but in the textile and coal industries wages were increased. At the end of 1915, for example, the *Ossett Observer* reported that miners' wages had risen 15.5 percent during the year with the result that their earnings had never been so high. Another source of friction was absenteeism. Among coal miners this does not seem to have been widespread but at the town's gas works it caused the manager problems. In 1916 he complained of his men constantly going from the works to drink and 'breaking time and leaving them in the lurch'.[13] The council responded by having the gas works put under the *Munitions Act* to make it easier for the manager to control his workers. Under the Act, for example, no employee in a certified works could change his job without an official permit.

There seems to have been only one strike in Ossett during the war. A strike among the Yorkshire miners in August 1918 led to all of the pits in Ossett being idle for a day. The issue in dispute was whether or not the meal hours of the surface men were included in their 54-hour week. To the *Ossett Observer* the strike was 'nothing less than a national disgrace'.[14]

To support the war effort there were numerous public and private initiatives in Ossett. From 1915 the mayor headed an annual subscription to raise money for Christmas gifts for the town's soldiers and sailors. The parcel sent to the servicemen abroad in that year contained cake, sweets, a pipe, tobacco, coffee, milk, chocolate, raisins and almonds. From August 1914 the mayoress chaired a committee to organise knitting and sewing for the troops. This brought a reproof from one reader of the *Ossett Observer* who criticised the ladies for taking work away from poorly paid garment workers.

The Mayoress' Bandaging Depot, set up in 1916, made bandages for military hospitals. Among those supplied was the new military hospital at Staincliffe in Dewsbury. A committee of ladies, chaired by the mayoress, raised funds in Ossett to buy 'extra nourishment' and 'comforts' for wounded soldiers in the hospital (Figure 4). To help equip the same institution, a group of lady wood workers, based at Pont-y-Garth in Station Road, turned out bed tables, back rests, foot rests, and crutches. Convalescing soldiers from local hospitals were also entertained in Ossett. One such event was in July 1916 when Southdale School presented a patriotic pageant, *Britannia Calls*, in the town hall.

Nursing was one practical way in which women could aid the war effort and within a month of the start of the conflict, a ladies' ambulance class was begun in the town. Of the 140 women who joined, 80 took the first-aid exam at its end and all passed. Some of the

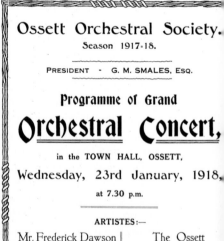

Ossett Orchestral Society.

Season 1917-18.

PRESIDENT - G. M. SMALES, ESQ.

Programme of Grand

Orchestral Concert,

in the TOWN HALL, OSSETT,

Wednesday, 23rd January, 1918,

at 7.30 p.m.

ARTISTES:—

Mr. Frederick Dawson
(Pianoforte).

Miss Esther Abson
(Soprano).

The Ossett
Orchestral Society.

Conductor: Mr. Harral Leach
F.I.G.C.M., F.V.C.M.
(By arrangement with the Directors of the Palladium, Ossett).

Madame JENNIE ARCHER, Accompanist.

THE NET PROCEEDS of this Concert will be handed over to The Ossett District Nursing Association, The S. John Ambulance Association, and The Soldiers' Comforts Fund Committee.

EDMUND LUND, F.S.A.A.,
Hon. Secretary.

Figure 4. Among the good causes supported by the Ossett Orchestral Society at its concert was the Soldiers' Comforts Fund Committee which provided 'extra nourishment' and 'comforts' for invalids at the Staincliffe military hospital.

members of the class went on in the following year to take a nursing course and all 48 of those who sat the exam passed, thus qualifying them to work in military hospitals as probationers.

When the war broke out there was a fear that it would create widespread unemployment. To alleviate the effects of this, the mayor started a local distress fund. The amount guaranteed to the fund stood at £225 by the end of August 1914, but as the disruption to Ossett's industry was only temporary, most of the calls on the fund came from the families of soldiers rather than the unemployed. In the following years there were frequent appeals for money to support war-related causes. The military hospital at Staincliffe, for example, was paid for from voluntary contributions from the townships making up the Dewsbury Poor Law Union. Ossett's share of the £6,000 needed was assessed at £430, but the town was able to raise £550.

To fund the war, the government raised direct and indirect taxes, but it also had to borrow huge amounts of money. Lending money to the government therefore became a patriotic act. Ossett's response, in the first two years of war, seems to have been generous: the Victory Loan launched at the beginning of 1917 raised £236,580 in the town. However in November of that year one of the leading figures in the war-savings movement in Ossett, Edmund Lund, noted that public interest in war savings was waning. Referring to the war savings associations which had been created to encourage the small investor, he claimed that workers felt that the more they saved with the government, the longer the war would last, and that the government would not keep its promise to exempt savings certificates from income tax. Only official assurances, he said, could restore confidence in government loans.

Lund's view that Ossett's war savings movement was flagging was borne out by the town's record in the last year of the war. In September 1917 the government started to issue National War Bonds with the avowed intention of meeting the cost of the war week by week without the need for another big loan. Unofficial targets based on population were set for towns and Ossett's weekly quota was set at £7,250. Ossett failed to fulfil this as by September 1918 only £162,710 had been subscribed rather than the £377,000 expected. The nearby towns of Wakefield and Dewsbury were more successful. Each raised 64% of its quota against Ossett's 43 per cent. This was despite two vigorous money-raising campaigns in 1918, one in February and the other in July. The former was publicised by a meeting in the town hall addressed by two MPs, speeches in the

Figure 5. The United Reformed Church was in 1914 the Sunday school of the Queen Street Primitive Methodists. Through their generosity Belgian refugees found a home there until the summer of 1915. *David Scriven.*

Palladium Cinema, a decorated tramcar, special illuminations and brass band performances in the Market Place.

Among those who benefited from fund raising in Ossett were Belgian refugees. The German invasion of Belgium, followed by the stories of German atrocities, evoked considerable sympathy for the refugees who fled to Britain. The Ossett corporation therefore arranged with the trustees of the Primitive Methodist chapel in Queen Street to house refugees in their Sunday School (Figure 5). In October 1914 two groups of refugees, totalling 79 people, arrived in the town. A few were accommodated in private houses, but most went to the Sunday School where Mrs I Willett acted as matron. Money to maintain the refugees was raised in the town by the Ossett Belgian Refugee Fund, but some of them soon found work and a scheme for dealing with their earnings was drawn up. Christmas 1914 was celebrated with a Christmas Eve party, a distribution of presents by Santa Claus and a Christmas dinner of roast beef and plum pudding.

Although the refugees generally received a warm welcome in Ossett, there was some criticism of both their treatment and their behaviour. They were, some critics claimed, too well fed and they drank too much. Certainly two of the men had to be sent to the refugee authorities in London because they refused to find paid work, would not make themselves useful at the Sunday School and encouraged others to follow their example. Such behaviour seems to have been exceptional as by the summer of 1915 almost all of the refugees who could work had found jobs, while some of the children were at school. At this point the 37 refugees who remained in the Sunday School were removed to seven cottages rented for them, a change welcomed by the refugees because it gave them greater independence. They remained in Ossett until 1919 when they returned to Belgium.

Food prices rose sharply at the outbreak of war, fell back, and then began to rise again. This upward movement was blamed by some on profiteering. In the view of William France, president of the Trades and Labour Council:

> *the capitalist would always take advantage of the poorer classes, and it was always the very poor who suffered first.*[15]

Members of the Chamber of Commerce had a more complex explanation which included speculation in wheat in the USA, high freight rates at sea, the requisitioning of ships by the government, and congestion on the British railways. Fixing maximum prices seemed to the Chamber the solution to the problem. Eventually in 1917 the government did regulate the prices of some foods, including bread. At the local level, price controls were enforced by food control committees. Ossett council appointed such a committee in August 1917 and it soon fixed retail prices for milk and meat.

Rising food prices reflected food shortages. To combat this situation a national voluntary food rationing programme was introduced in February 1917. In Ossett the members of the Chamber of Commerce tried to set an example by pledging to observe the officially recommended rations. A number of shops in the town also implemented voluntary rationing with the Co-operative Society restricting sugar purchases according to the number of people in the family. Voluntary rationing was not, however, a success. Shortages encouraged the hoarding of food and it was easy to evade the Co-op's restrictions by making purchases in several shops.

Scarcity of tea, butter and margarine led in the winter of 1917-18 to long queues outside shops. At the Maypole Dairy it was necessary to wait two or three hours to buy 8oz of margarine. As many adults could not afford this time, children were sent to queue, leading to a dip in attendance at the town's schools. Shortages led to industrial unrest. At the beginning of 1918 it was rumoured that unless supplies improved, 2,000 workers would go on strike in the town.

The failure of voluntary rationing made compulsory schemes inevitable. Ossett's Food Control Committee introduced its own scheme for rationing butter, margarine and tea in January 1918, while national rationing of sugar and meat came into force in Ossett in January and April 1918 respectively. Rationing was so unpopular with some workers that there were threats to break every window in the town hall.

The growing food crisis encouraged the development of the allotment movement. The council began by providing 27 allotments off Wesley Street in January 1917, but by March 1918 it was letting over 300 holdings on sites scattered throughout the town. To protect their interests, the tenants formed the Ossett and District Allotment Society Limited. The Society had the power to rent and purchase land and to supply chemicals and fertilisers and offered its members mutual protection against trespassers. Allotment holders were encouraged by two series of talks on gardening, one in 1917 and the other in 1918, given by lecturers from Leeds University. The gardeners needed encouragement as not only was the local soil poor for potatoes, one of the crops they were urged to grow, but the winter of 1916-17 was exceptionally long and hard.

The food crisis gave the temperance movement another argument for prohibition: barley was being wasted to make beer. In 1918 the local temperance workers took part in a national campaign to introduce prohibition into the country for the duration of the war and during demobilisation. A poll held in the town in May resulted in a large majority in favour of the proposal: 4,576 votes were for prohibition and 979 against. Although the prohibitionists never achieved their aim, restrictions on the opening times of public houses were introduced to discourage absenteeism from work. Absenteeism does not seem to have been a major problem in Ossett, but in February 1915 the town's licensing justices limited the sale of drink to between 6.00am and 9.00pm. Not surprisingly the Dewsbury and District Licensed Victuallers' Association protested against the restrictions. In its view they were unfair to workers because those working overtime were unable to go to public houses after work, and unfair to publicans because trade had already been adversely affected by the war. In addition, it claimed that drunkenness was not a problem in the Dewsbury area. Their protests went unheeded and in November 1915 further restrictions were introduced in the West Riding, with opening hours confined on weekdays to 12 noon to 2.30pm and 6.30pm to 9.30pm while on Sundays they were 12.30pm to 2.30pm and 6.00pm to 9.00pm. Shorter opening hours, increased beer duties and weaker beers all contributed to a decline in convictions for drunkenness in the town from twenty-one in 1914-1915 to nine in 1917-1918. Although this was pleasing to the licensing justices, their chairman, Henry Westwood, expressed concern in 1917 at a considerable increase of drinking among soldiers' wives. Westwood may have been right, but accusations that soldiers' wives drank excessively were common during the war and were often unfounded.

The summer of 1918 was particularly difficult in Ossett. Rationing of some foods had been introduced, but shortages continued to affect the town. At the end of August there was a dearth of yeast with the result that bread was unobtainable in some shops. During the same week there were complaints about the meat in the butchers' shops: most of it was frozen and of a poor quality. Nature inflicted further hardship on the town. A prolonged local drought led to water rationing for industrial and domestic consumers in August. Heavy rains in the following month ended rationing but were followed by flooding in the Calder valley. Ossett was also affected by the influenza epidemic which claimed 150,000 lives in England and Wales in 1918-19. To hinder the spread of the disease Ossett's schools were closed on three occasions in July, July-August, and November. Sunday Schools were also closed and restrictions were placed on children attending the Palladium Cinema. However influenza killed 32 people in the town in 1918 and another 24 in 1919, while pneumonia, which was linked to influenza, took 34 victims in 1918 and 24 in 1919.[16] This accumulation of hardships contributed to a growing war weariness in the town that alarmed some citizens (Figure 6). At a meeting of the Chamber of Commerce in July, J Ward warned that many people were becoming inclined to 'peace at any price' and urged that 'something ought to be done to put a stop to it.'[17] He proposed that the Chamber should counter defeatist talk by publicising the war aims of the Allies.

By this time the German armies in France had failed in their last

Figure 6. On 19 November 1918 an RAF biplane flying from Doncaster to Newcastle on Tyne lost its was in fog and crashed in a field near Wesley Street. Luckily the pilot, Lieutenant Taylor, was unhurt.

attempts to break the Allies. As the Allied forces counter-attacked, the Germans began a retreat that ended with the signing of the armistice on Monday 11 November. Rumours of the armistice were confirmed by a telephone call to the Ossett town clerk's office at 11.30am, half-an-hour after it had come into force on the Western Front. The immediate response of the small group of official and corporation members gathered there was to sing the national anthem. Then the town hall bells were rung and rockets were fired from the fire station to alert the town to the good news. Mill buzzers joined in the noisy celebration and hundreds of patriotic flags quickly appeared in the streets.

The remainder of the day, except in the coal mines, became an unofficial holiday. In the early afternoon the mayor, Alderman Wilson, read the official telegram announcing the armistice to a large crowd in the Market Place. Later, in the evening, Wilson lit a large bonfire that had been built in Gedham Field, and distributed fireworks to children. The Ossett and Gawthorpe bands paraded the streets.

There was a more serious note to the celebrations. During the evening, services of thanksgiving were held in a number of churches. At Holy Trinity church an impressive service was conducted by Reverend R E Burlingham. Among the hymns sung by a large congregation were *O God, Our Help in Ages Past* and *Now Thank We All Our God*, while there was also an organ rendition of the *Hallelujah Chorus*.

For many, of course, the armistice came too late. The families of the 230 Ossett men killed during the war might feel relief that the conflict was over, but would bear the burden of their loss for years to come.

Notes and References

Two recent introductions to Britain's experience in the First World War are *The First World War in British History*, (1995), edited by S Constantine, M W Kirby and M B Rose, and *Blighty: British Society in the Era of the Great War*, (1996), by G J DeGroot. Most of the material in this essay comes from the *Ossett Observer* and the *Wakefield Express*.

1. *Ossett Observer*, 15 August 1914.
2. *Ibid*, 5 September 1914.
3. *Ibid*, 29 January 1916.
4. *Ibid*, 19 February 1916.
5. *Wakefield Express*, 27 October 1917.
6. Holy Trinity Infant School log book, 8 March 1917, West Yorkshire Archive Service, Wakefield. WMD/4/2/32/3.
7. Christ Church Infant School log book, 17 March 1916, West Yorkshire Archive Service, Wakefield, WMD/4/2/8/1.
8. *Ossett Observer* 15 May 1915.
9. *Ibid*, 8 January 1916.
10. *Ibid*, 24 October 1914.
11. See the essay on Lofthouse Park by Peter Wood in *Aspects of Wakefield* (1998).
12. *Ossett Observer* 28 April 1917.
13. *Ossett Observer*, 11 November 1916.
14. *Ibid*, 24 August 1918.
15. *Ibid*, 23 January 1915.
16. Report of the Medical Officer for Health for 1918, Table III
    Report of the Medical Officer for Health for 1919, Table III
    West Yorkshire Archive Service, WMT/05/6/1/3.
17. *Ossett Observer* 27 July 1918.

4. In Place of the Stork: Maternity Provision in Wakefield

by Kate Taylor

AT THE BEGINNING OF THE TWENTIETH CENTURY it was the norm for women to give birth either in their own homes or at the house of a close relative. Certainly in Wakefield almost every birth was in a private house. Occasionally a child was born in Clayton Hospital, or in the Asylum (later known as Stanley Royd Hospital) and a modest number were born in the workhouse which the superintendent, when he registered their births, discreetly identified only as 90 Park Lodge Lane. Although infant mortality had been dropping throughout most of the nineteenth century it was still comparatively high and in Wakefield in 1900 stood at one in fifty.

The first step towards better maternity care in Wakefield came in 1903 with the appointment by the Wakefield Sanitary Aid Society, a body which attributed infant deaths in part to poor-quality housing and in part to ignorance on the part of mothers, of a health visitor in

Figure 1. Manygates child welfare centre, 1999. *Kate Taylor.*

the shape of Miss Boileau. In 1906 she founded *Babies Welcome*, the first organisation of its kind in the country. This was initially a provident society, encouraging pregnant women themselves to save money towards buying baby clothes and other necessities, but later it also made grants to those in need. Wakefield Corporation employed its own health visitor from 1908 although her responsibilities extended beyond those of mother-and-baby care and she served as the school nurse. When Miss Boileau left in 1910, Wakefield appointed a second health visitor. By 1929 it had six.

The city's first child welfare centre was opened on 15 April 1912, in a room in the town hall. In 1915 it moved to the old coffee tavern in Kirkgate, in 1917 to the soup kitchen in Almshouse Lane and in 1918 to the Primitive Methodist Chapel Sunday school in Market Street. In 1915 two further centres were opened, at the Homestead on Alverthorpe Road, and at the Patriotic Club, Haddingley Hill, Sandal. This latter centre moved a year later to the Primitive Methodist Chapel Sunday school in Doncaster Road where it remained until the purpose-built centre was opened in the grounds of Manygates on Barnsley Road in 1935 (Figure 1). A fourth Child Welfare Centre was established in 1916 in St John's Mission Room in Providence Street and in 1917 a fifth centre was opened at Eastmoor in the Wesleyan Chapel Sunday school. Volunteers from *Babies Welcome* assisted at the clinics.

But still childbirth itself took place in the home. In his report for 1917-1918, the city's Medical Officer of Health, Thomas Gibson, pointed out that there were only fifteen midwives in the city and that only five of those were trained; two were available only, in one case, to the patients of one particular doctor and, in the other, to the wives of employees of one particular Wakefield firm. In all the midwives attended at only half of the confinements. He wrote in the report:

> *At present the great blank in the local midwifery services is the absence of a maternity hospital. The only maternity wards in the city are in the Poor Law Infirmary and these are used mainly for the confinement of unmarried women. Patients are only admitted to the Infirmary by an order from the Relieving Officer and, needless to say, the Poor Law Infirmary may be ruled out as providing accommodation for the General Public. Confinement cases are occasionally admitted to Clayton Hospital but these are nearly always complicated cases requiring surgical assistance. From my experience I have no hesitation in saying that there is a great need for the provision of a maternity hospital in Wakefield.*

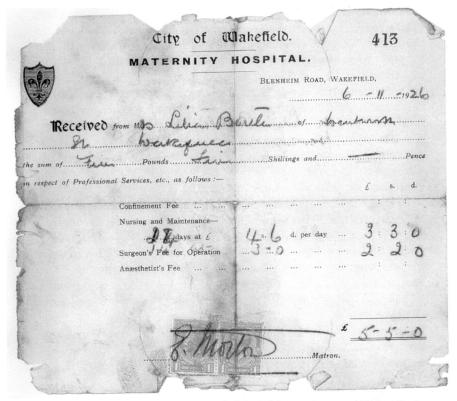

Figure 2. Bill for encouchement at St John's Mount. *Courtesy of Michael Bartle.*

Dr Gibson argued that two types of case would benefit in particular: those women whose homes were 'unsatisfactory' and who could not have the necessary attention during the period of lying-in, and those where a difficult birth was anticipated. He recommended the choice of site for the hospital in a quiet place, away from the main traffic, but as near as possible to the city centre.

But before the report was presented his advice had already been taken. In November 1917, during the First World War, Dr Gibson submitted a scheme to establish a maternity hospital, central child welfare centre and ante-natal clinic. A month later the authority's Mental Deficiency and Child Welfare Committee - the body that was to remain responsible for maternity provision until the creation of the National Health Service in 1948 - recommended the purchase of St John's Mount, a large house in Blenheim Road (Figures 2 and 3).

The house had been built in the late 1880s, on the newly-developing estate, by the Wakefield worsted-spinner, W T Marriott (1822-1899) for his son-in-law, Andrew Chalmers (1840-1912), minister at Westgate Chapel from 1880-1909. A contract to buy the property from Marriott's son, William Hall Marriott, for £2,250 was agreed in May 1918 and the authority took over furniture and fittings for a further £105 3s 6d. Local firms were employed to undertake the conversion: H Gillott of Cheapside (plumbing), Percy Parker, Northgate (electric wiring), and Charles Turner and Son (painting and decorating). Eight 'Lawson Tait' spring bedsteads at £3 4s 9d each, and six cots at £3 2s each were ordered from Stephensons Ltd. The closure of the wartime military hospital at Heath brought other appropriate articles to St John's Mount.

In October 1918 the authority appointed Charlotte Dickson, then at Great Ormond Street Children's Hospital, London, as the matron, at a salary of £80 a year, which was raised to £100 a year later. Fees for the mothers were to be 10s (50p) a day plus a further 2s (10p) for maintenance. Women could be admitted from other parts of the West Riding at a rate of £2 2s (£2 20p) per week. Any woman who booked to have her baby at the hospital was expected to attend ante-natal clinics there.

The first patient was admitted on 9 April 1919. In the first year there were 62 admissions. Charlotte Dickson was followed as matron in 1921 by H J More and she was succeeded in 1923 by Edith Morton.

The 1920s saw rapidly increasing numbers of women electing to give birth in the maternity hospital rather than at home and in 1931 there were 410 admissions. In 1928 Dr Jessie Eeles, then at the

Figure 3. St John's Mount: Wakefield's first maternity hospital, 1999. *Kate Taylor.*

Figure 4. Margaret Street child welfare centre, 1999. *Kate Taylor.*

Maternity Hospital, Acomb, York, was appointed as Wakefield's assistant medical officer and the first doctor to be charged specifically with care of the ante-natal clinic, the maternity hospital and child welfare centres. Her initial salary was £600. In December 1931 Kate Perkins, of 42 Hyde Terrace, Leeds, was appointed matron at £140 a year.

Meanwhile further child welfare centres had been opened in other parts of the city. In 1919 a centre was opened in Mark Street in Christ Church Mission Room. The Hatfeild Street centre closed in 1920 and a new one was opened at Alverthorpe in the Wesleyan Chapel Sunday School. But by 1927 Dr Gibson was increasingly dissatisfied with child-welfare provision. In his annual report he observed:

> It is not necessary to reiterate the importance of maternity and child welfare work. This being so, it does seem extraordinary that to a large extent this important work is carried out in premises not adapted to the purposes and in some instances quite unsuitable.

The answer was, he believed, for the authority to have a central building of its own. The following year Wakefield Corporation bought the Cliffe, a substantial house in Margaret Street and it came into use on 6 January 1930 as the principal child welfare centre (Figure 4). Its formal opening was performed by Dame Janet Campbell. The only other centres to remain open were at Belle Vue and at Alverthorpe. However the development of the Lupset housing estate led to the opening of a child welfare centre at Snapethorpe Hall in the early 1930s.

It was the 1929 *Local Government Act* that necessitated more extensive provision by Wakefield Corporation for maternity care. The Ministry of Health enquired whether additional accommodation could be found either at the Wakefield Union Infirmary (the workhouse) in Park Lodge Lane, which was taken over by the West Riding County Council and became the White Rose Hospital and later the County General Hospital, or at Clayton Hospital.

The Authority's answer was to look for a better site for its own, more extensive, maternity hospital and by January 1931 consent had been obtained from the Ministry of Health to obtain a loan of £2,500 to buy Manygates House and its grounds from Archdeacon Richard Phipps (Figure 5). The house had been built for Edward Green about 1845. Phipps had moved there in the 1920s, buying it from Thomas Percy Tew. The house was enlarged and a new two-storey block, designed by city architect Louis Ives, was built to provide thirty-five beds. The foundation stone of the new block was laid by Councillor Fanny W Stott on 16 March 1934 (Figures 6 and 7) Kate Perkins remained to become the matron of the new hospital. Dr Jessie Eeles moved there as the resident medical officer.

Manygates Hospital was opened by the mayor of Wakefield, then Councillor F W T Mills, on 9 October 1935.

Initially the authority planned to convert St John's Mount into Public Assistance offices but there were strong objections from local residents and in March 1938 its sale was agreed, the proceeds being applied to reducing the debt on Manygates.

The County General Hospital continued to have a maternity ward. The Wakefield area gained a further maternity hospital, at Walton Hall, in 1942. The hall had been requisitioned as a military hospital in 1940 but it was quickly recognised that it was unsuitable. Thus it was put by the West Riding County Council to another unsuitable use, bearing in mind that access is by boat or footbridge only (Figure 8). The first baby was born there on 14 June.

In July 1948, with the creation of the National Health Service, responsibility for Manygates passed to the new Wakefield Group A Hospital Management Committee. The last meeting of Wakefield's Mental and Child Welfare Committee was held on 8 June when its long-standing chairman, Councillor Mrs Effie Crowe, was warmly thanked for all her work.

Walton Hall also came under the control of the Group A Hospital Management Committee, together with Clayton Hospital, the County General Hospital, Oulton Hall, Cardigan Sanatorium, Snapethorpe Isolation Hospital, Carr Gate, and Hatfeild Hall. (The Wakefield B Group embraced only Stanley Royd and Pinderfields hospitals.)

John McKiddie came to Manygates as consultant obstetrician

Figure 5. Manygates House, 1999.
Kate Taylor.

Figure 6. Stone laid by Councillor Fanny W Stott. *Kate Taylor.*

in the 1950s and remained for some thirty years.

With the completion of extensions at Manygates Hospital, in December 1966, it was at last possible to close Walton Hall as a maternity home. The extensions cost £189,000 and brought the number of maternity beds up to 73. They were opened formally by the Countess of Scarborough on 11 March 1967 and dedicated by the Bishop of Wakefield, John A Ramsbotham. The matron at the time was K Barbour.

The outpatients department was upgraded in 1986-7 with ten new examination rooms and was re-opened by Sir Jack Smart on 1 May 1987.

But a very few years later the radical scheme to transfer maternity provision to Pinderfields Hospital was mooted. Manygates Hospital

Figure 7. The 1935 maternity block at Manygates. *Kate Taylor.*

Figure 8. Walton Hall.

closed on 12 December 1992. The last baby born there was Marcus Tyson who was moved, with his mother, to Pinderfields when he was just two hours old. The first baby to be born at Pinderfields was Olivia Charlotte Padget whose mother had been a midwife at Manygates.

The name of Manygates has been preserved in the title of the Manygates Maternity Unit at Pinderfields. The suite comprises a labour ward, a post-natal ward, an ante-natal ward, a special care unit and an ante-natal clinic.

The Manygates complex was sold to Bretton Hall College in 1995 and, after substantial residential accommodation had been built, students moved into the new 'village' there in September 1996. The former ante-natal centre and child welfare clinic is in 1999 an access and training unit run by Bretton Hall and providing training, primarily in information technology, for both college students and local companies.

Whilst Manygates, and later Pinderfields, catered for the great majority of mothers-to-be, there were, in the middle years of the century, births in private nursing homes and maternity homes. These were never many in number. The medical officer's report for 1927 shows that there were 234 births at St John's Mount, 41 at the White Rose Hospital (the workhouse) and only twenty in private institutions. Some few births took place in the 1920s and 1930s in a private nursing home at 2 St John's North. This is shown in the 1922 trade directory as the 'trained nurses' home' with Alice Pollard as its principal. However from 1926 - or possible earlier - it was run as a nursing home by Edith Goodrick and Evelyn Wyld. It closed about 1938 and the house became a family home.

By 1926 there was a private nursing home, known as Silverdale, at St John's Terrace, Margaret Street. The nursing home was in a block of houses owned, by copyhold of the Manor of Wakefield, until 1919 by John Henry Holdsworth and then by his son, Ernest. The premises were rented initially by Mrs Nellie Kirk; she was followed in about 1930 by Florence Mary Holmes and Elizabeth Hargreaves. Here were born the children of the middle classes whose fathers included, for example, an accountant, an architect, a butcher, a work's manager, a bank clerk, a colliery clerk and a secondary school master. The nursing home was extended by 1934 to take in the adjoining house. There was accommodation for six or eight mothers primarily in individual rooms. In the 1940s it was run by Honora Delahunty with assistance from a Sister Johnson, Ruby Jaques, Agnes Devine and Emily Hodgson (Figure 9). Mothers each had their own room and were allowed as many visitors as they wanted. Fees in the 1940s were £15 a week. The mother's own doctor attended the confinement where necessary. Honora Delahuny bought both No. 1 and No. 3 Margaret Street in 1946 She sold No. 3 Margaret Street in 1949 to Wakefield Corporation and the adjoining

Figure 9 Bill for Silverdale.
Courtesy of Joyce Denning.

property, again to the Corporation, in 1954. The terrace was later demolished to make way for new buildings for what is now Wakefield College.

Sister Johnson moved to Horbury to run a maternity home in Benton Hill. This closed in the 1960s. In Milnthorpe Lane, Nurse Edith Bailey ran a modest maternity unit, catering for one or two people at a time, in Ramleh, one of six semi-detached houses which

Figure 10. Ramleh, the maternity home run by Nurse Bailey, 1999. *Kate Taylor.*

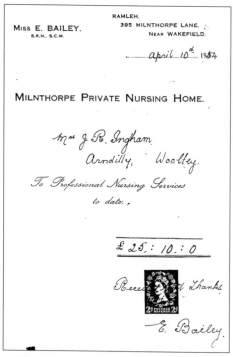

MISS E. BAILEY.
S.R.N., S.C.M.

RAMLEH.
395 MILNTHORPE LANE.
NEAR WAKEFIELD.

April 10th 1954

MILNTHORPE PRIVATE NURSING HOME.

Mrs J Ro. Ingham.
Arndilly, Woolley.

To Professional Nursing Services
to date.

£ 25 : 10 : 0

Received with Thanks

E. Bailey.

Figure 11. Bill for Nurse Bailey's maternity home. *Courtesy of Mary Ingham.*

had been built by Edward Green and sons for their employees (Figures 10 and 11). Miss Bailey was the firm's nurse and acted as midwife to employees' wives. She bought the house, with the help of a £500 mortgage from Green's, in 1926. She added a flat-roofed extension with bedrooms coloured in pink or blue, allocated on the basis of the baby's sex. A brother lived next door. Nurse Bailey was still running her nursing home in the early 1960s. Her uniform is said to have been very old-fashioned with a large headdress and skirts almost down to the floor. Her sister acted as the housekeeper and cook, grew vegetables in the garden and made her own bread. The sisters cycled into Wakefield on Saturday afternoons to do their shopping. One mother who gave birth there in 1954 recalls Miss Bailey's practice of cleaning the bedroom linoleum by putting down tea leaves which she then swept up. Another recalled being served a - in her condition quite inedible - bloater for breakfast. Here too the woman's own doctor delivered the baby where necessary.

Nurse Bailey was highly valued by people living in the neighbourhood as she was ever ready to deal with their nursing needs, whether to bandage a child's knee or to attend a stroke victim regularly twice a day.

Acknowledgments

I should like to thank Wakefield's Superintendent Registrar, and the members of the public who contacted me in response to a letter in the *Wakefield Express* for their help in providing information.

Sources

Thomas Gibson, *Notes on Public Health in Wakefield in the Nineteenth Century and from 1901-1935.*
Peter Wright, *A History of Walton*, 1986.
Wakefield Corporation Council Minutes.
Trade directories.
Register of Electors.
Medical Officers' Annual Reports.
The *Wakefield Express.*

5. PORTOBELLO: WAKEFIELD'S FIRST MAJOR COUNCIL HOUSING ESTATE

by Angela Petyt

BY THE SEVENTEENTH CENTURY Wakefield was the administrative centre of the West Riding of Yorkshire. As the town grew in stature so did the population. Old yards filled the centre (originally medieval burgage plots) in which were crammed houses and other buildings. Two hundred years later conditions were extremely unhealthy. There were 62 deaths from cholera in 1832, although twenty of these were at the prison, and in 1849 more than 100 inhabitants died from cholera. In 1893, 744 people died from typhoid and related diseases. The Kirkgate, Eastmoor and Westgate Common areas were particularly notorious. Something had to be done to protect the health of the people of Wakefield. The *Housing Acts* of 1890 and 1919 gave local authorities the right to clear slum areas and to re-house the tenants in council-built homes, subject to approval from the Ministry of Health. Wakefield, with its crowded yards, was in dire need of new housing. Created a municipal borough in 1848, a city in 1888, and a county borough in 1915, Wakefield needed to look the part, which meant clearing up the over-populated centre. However, it must be noted that Wakefield was quite late in comparison with other local authorities in implementing a slum-clearance and re-housing policy. It was only in 1918 that the Labour-run council, headed by George Blakey, set about the task. In 1919 a Housing and Town Planning Committee was set up, which met once a month to discuss the new council housing schemes. Between the wars, many of the old slums were demolished and large estates of local authority houses were built, away from the city centre. Therefore, the boundaries of Wakefield spread further outwards and the city began to live up to its status with a cleaner, more spacious centre, and new, healthy housing estates for its citizens.

COUNCIL ESTATES BUILT BY WAKEFIELD CORPORATION 1918-1939

Name	Begun
Portobello	1921
Lupset	1924
Eastmoor	1930
Darnley	1930
Peacock Farm	1936
Flanshaw	1936

Figure 1. View of Portobello Road, 1999. *Angela Petyt.*

The first known mention of the site in Wakefield around the area now called Portobello was in the Manor Court Rolls of 1339. It is referred to in 1340 as 'a place called Pokenale, which land was acquired by the overflowing of the water'. This refers to the Pugneys, low ground by the River Calder, about 1.5 miles south of Wakefield city centre, in the parish of Sandal Magna. On 30 December 1460, during the Wars of the Roses, a major battle took place in the area including Pugneys and what is now Manygates Park between the Yorkists, based at nearby Sandal Castle, and the Lancastrians, based at Pontefract Castle. Richard Plantagenet, Duke of York, lost his life. About the year 1800, most of the common fields around Sandal Magna were enclosed under the terms of the Inclosure Act 1799. During the nineteenth century the extensive parish comprised numerous hamlets, including Milnthorpe, Woodthorpe, Agbrigg and Pledwick. Sandal village was on the main route from Wakefield to London. A primarily agricultural area, there were also a number of large houses in Sandal, owned by wealthy families. One such residence was Portobello House, built in 1825 for Joseph Holdsworth. The house was named after Porto Bello in Panama - the most important port in South America in colonial times. A battle was fought there between the occupying Spanish and the British in 1739, won by the latter. When the foundations of the house were dug, human bones, broken swords, spurs and fragments of armour from the Battle of Wakefield were found. There were extensive gardens, said to have been laid out by Joseph Paxton. Being set away from the main road, close to the river, the house was hidden from view. Before

1918, Portobello was mainly a quiet, grassy area. However, there were the large Calder Mills and Castle Bank Mills on Portobello Road, and a group of Edwardian terraces named after events in the Boer War - Acme, Abbott, Kimberly, Pretoria and Emblem (Figure 1). From the highest point in the fields, one had a good view of Wakefield. It was bordered by the ancient thoroughfare of Cock and Bottle Lane, by now re-named Manygates Lane, after an old close called Mannygaites mentioned in the Manor Court Rolls of 1676. Long-term resident of Portobello and Sandal, Mrs Phyllis Bell, recollects when:

> *It was all fields and there was a gate across the lane to let the farm animals in and out. One year, when there was an epidemic of diphtheria, our school took us all to Portobello to have our lessons sat on the hill in the fresh air. It was a nice place, with lovely views over the Pugneys.*

After the Housing and Town Planning Act was passed in 1919, Wakefield Corporation set about the construction of a full-scale housing estate, having experimented with houses on Elm Tree Street (Belle Vue) and Rufford Street (Alverthorpe) in 1920. It was decided in that year to purchase land at Portobello from the owners of Portobello House, Mrs Ada Gascoigne and Mrs Edith Colvin, leaving the house and gardens intact. The Housing and Town Planning Committee was headed by Councillor Graham. The Corporation was caught between the Ministry of Health and the Wakefield Master Builders' Federation. Under the 1919 Act tenders had to be submitted to the Ministry of Health before the local authority could accept them. But when the Corporation put the work out for competition, the Federation complained as it expected to be awarded the contact as had been the case with the houses on Rufford Street. Opportunities for local builders were scarce in this immediate post-war period and the Federation was anxious to secure the interests of its members. The tender for the first 76 houses was to be used as a yardstick for the rest of the scheme. There would be electric lighting and gas for cooking. There would also be provision for coal fires in the living room and the largest bedroom. A tender was submitted in November 1920 for 76 houses at Portobello by the Builders' Federation. The Corporation accepted it subject to the approval of the Ministry. But this was withheld, the area Housing Commissioner, T E Marr, advising that the local authority must seek tenders from a wider circle of builders or consider employing direct labour. The streets and sewers were also being constructed at this time (February 1921) and were at a sufficiently advanced stage to allow the houses to be built. The Corporation had given the navvies working on the streets and sewers a 4d (1.67p) per hour rise, but again the Ministry of Health did not approve insisting that they should be classed as 'public works contractors' labourers' and not 'builders' labourers'. The unemployed and ex-servicemen were employed on the Portobello scheme. In April the Ministry rejected the estimates for Contract No. 1 (the 76 houses). They also set initial rents:

Type A　Living room, scullery, two bedrooms　　　　　　8s 0d (40p)
Type A　Living room, scullery, three bedrooms　　　　　10s 0d (50p)
Type B　Living room, scullery, parlour, three bedrooms　12s 6d (62.5p)
　　　　　　(Per week, excluding rates and water charges)

In May 1921 the Corporation submitted to the Ministry of Health a request for a loan of £37,604 for the Portobello scheme. As Contract No. 1 had been rejected by the Ministry, the Corporation invited tenders from individual members of the Master Builders' Federation. Added to this problem was the reduction of wages for craftsmen and labourers by 2d (0.83p) and 3d (1.23p) per hour respectively, which did not meet with approval from the workers.

Messrs R McAlpine submitted a tender for 300 houses, but the Ministry of Health again blocked the plan, stating that they would only agree to the erection of 50 houses at the prices quoted. It also said that, to reduce costs, the houses could be made smaller. Messrs Elvey & Steel submitted a tender for 50 houses with the average cost of a Type A house being £624 5s. 4d., and a Type B houses costing £710 13s. 8d and this was accepted. The Committee urgently wanted a meeting with the Minister of Health to discuss the desperate need for houses in Wakefield, and how they required financial aid to build sufficient houses to solve the problem (Figures 2 - 4).

Figure 2. Type 'A' houses on Warren Avenue, 1999. *Angela Petyt.*

Figure 3. Type 'B' parlour houses on Rutland Avenue, 1999. *Angela Petyt.*

A tender from Messrs G Crook for 40 houses was accepted in August. The Corporation at that time was purchasing bricks direct from Wilson's kiln at the end of Newland Street, Agbrigg, at 83s (£4 15p) per thousand, to which the Ministry of Health objected strongly, saying it should buy them from the DBMS.

While the building was going on in the autumn of 1921, Wakefield Ladies' Hockey Club used part of the Portobello site as a pitch, which was one of a number of schemes devised by the Corporation to raise money - such as selling off the turf, and using other parts of the area for grazing animals.

An electricity sub-station was built on the estate in 1922 to supply power to the houses. A decision was made to install a wall plug in the houses for the use of an electric cooking ring or iron. The Corporation also purchased kitchen ranges and mantles from local ironmongers, at prices set by the DBMS., learning their lesson from the 'bricks affair'.

The layout plan of Portobello Estate was shown to the Committee by the Housing Architect. It contained a site for shops, which the Corporation discovered would not receive a subsidy from the government. It was decided to advertise the shops for sale in the private sector (Figure 5).

In January 1922 the weekly rents for Portobello were set at 9s (45p) for a Type A house and 11s (55p) for a Type B house. This was not carried unanimously by the Committee, and, after a heated

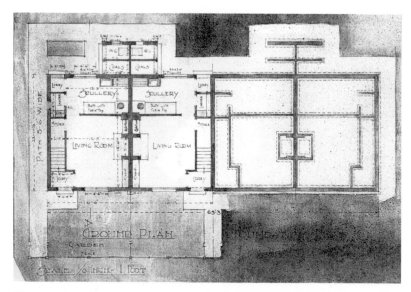

Figure 4. Architect's plan of houses, with bath downstairs in the scullery, and outside   lavatory. West Yorkshire Archive Service, Wakefield, C861. *Courtesy of WMDC Education Dept, Museums and Arts.*

debate, it was agreed that checks would be made on similar houses in Wakefield to see what the landlords charged under the *1919 Act*. A house in nearby Acme Terrace, which could be compared to a Type A house, cost 6s 2d (30.83p), and had no bath. The rents for

Figure 5. Portobello Estate aerial photograph, c1926, West Yorkshire Archive Service, Wakefield, B280, Wakefield City Engineer's papers. *Courtesy of WMDC Library and Information Services: Local Studies.*

Portobello were duly changed to 8s (40p) and 10s (50p)

The layout plan for the shops' site was sent to the Ministry of Health in February 1922 for approval. In March, the first applicants were offered tenancies of houses on Portobello. The families came mainly from the nearby Belle Vue area, where overcrowding and unhealthy living conditions were rife. The Ministry stated that no rents should be lower than 8s 6d (42.5p) and 10s 6d (52.5p) per week, and therefore Portobello rents were changed yet again. The naming of the streets was considered and in June 1922 it was decided to name them thus:

Duke of York Avenue	named after Richard Plantagenet, Duke of York, killed at the Battle of Wakefield in 1460
Clifford Avenue	named after Lord 'Bloody' Clifford,
Clifford View	murderer of both the Duke of York and his son, Edmund, at the Battle of Wakefield
Warren Avenue	named after the Earls Warrenne, Lords of the Manor of Wakefield 1090-1347
Castle Avenue	named after nearby Sandal Castle, headquarters of the Manor of Wakefield
Rutland Avenue	named after Edmund, Earl of Rutland, killed after the Battle of Wakefield by Lord Clifford (Figure 6)

It was proposed that 56 more houses should be built to house tenants who would be made homeless by the clearing of the Volunteer Yard insanitary area. Pincheon Street was also to be demolished under the Wakefield Improvement Scheme. Both were situated off Kirkgate. Therefore 110 houses needed to be built in the next phase. 40 of these would rank for a government subsidy, as long as the Corporation built 40 without financial assistance.

More land was needed for the extra houses and was bought from

Figure 6. View of Warren Avenue, 1999. *Angela Petyt.*

the owners of Portobello House by the Corporation. The extra streets were named thus:

Hastings Avenue	named after Sir Hugh Hastings, killed at the Battle of Wakefield
Pugneys Road	named after the land that it overlooks the Pugneys
Portobello Road) Portobello Grove)	named after Portobello House

In April 1923, the tenant of 23 Duke of York Avenue, wished to sell tobacco from his house, as many people had sold various goods from their homes in the slums. He was refused, and the Corporation issued notice that anyone who sold goods in such a way would be evicted. In July, the Corporation received notice from the Ministry of

Figure 7. The *Portobello Hotel*, 1999. *Angela Petyt.*

Health stating they could borrow £1,810 for street works, £490 for fencing and £23,496 for 76 houses under Part III of the *Housing of the Working Classes Act 1890*. The Ministry also approved the sale of four shop sites at £700 each, which were eventually occupied by a greengrocer's, butcher's, grocer's, and a newsagent. A branch of the Wakefield Industrial Co-operative Society was situated on Portobello Road, and a wooden hut was used as a fish and chip shop by Herbert Robinson. More tenancies were offered, the particulars of some being noted in the Housing and Town Planning Committee minutes of October 1923:

(B.2297)	Man, wife, four children and grandmother. Living in house required by landlord, whose family of five sleep in one bedroom. Resident of Wakefield. No army service. Applied October 1922 - offered tenancy of a Type B house on Portobello.
(C.431)	Man, wife and five children in lodgings. Sleeping in one bedroom. Wakefield resident ex-serviceman. Applied March 1920 - offered tenancy of a Type A House on Portobello.

The final accounts were submitted in October 1923 for Contracts 1 and 2. The approved price for Contract 1 was £32,650 6s. 8d., plus £1,190 for additional work. The final cost was £32,939 10s. 9d - a saving of £710 15s. 11d. A saving was also made on Contract 2.

In 1924 a public house was built on Portobello Road and named

Figure 8. Manygates School and the Duke of York memorial, 1999. *Angela Petyt*

Figure 9. The Duke of York memorial when first erected in 1897.

the Portobello Hotel (Figure 7). It was also decided to build an elementary school on a triangular piece of land comprising five acres, bordered by Milnthorpe Lane and Manygates Lane, and alongside the Duke of York Memorial (erected 1897) (Figures 8 and 9). Messrs G Crook and Sons won the contract and built the school at a cost of £37,000. In November 1928, Manygates School was opened by Lord Lascelles of Harewood (Figures 10 - 11). The number of pupils on roll would be 480 in the Senior department, and 350 in the Junior department. Portobello House was occupied by the Mayor of 1926, a popular local man, George Henry Sherwood, and his family from 1925 - 1935, when it was purchased by S C Smith. (In 1956 the house was demolished and the Riverside Villas erected on the site.)

Mrs Phyllis Bell moved into 17 Warren Avenue in 1925, when she was 17 years old:

When we first moved to Warren Avenue, the houses which now stand across the street were only just being built. The house had a very large garden, with open fields at the back. At the rear of the house was a porch which had a door for the coal, a door for the toilet and a door to the scullery, which had a sink in the corner, a bath under a table top, and a pantry. There was a through lounge with a cast iron range where all the cooking was done, and three bedrooms, one with a coal fire. It was a nice house on a nice estate. You were thought to be really lucky if you got a house on Portobello.

When fully built by the end of the 1920s, Portobello was a well-designed estate, with 540 houses, four shops, a school and a public house. In addition to Elvey and Steel, and George Crook, building contractors included Newton and Barnes, Ellis and Longbottom, J

Figure 10. Laying the foundation stone for Manygates School, 1926. *C Brooke*

Hancock, J Woodhead, A and H Fisk, and A Saville. Electrical work was undertaken by Walter Robb and W A Beaumont. Sinks were provided by the Farnley Iron Co.

A garden-city approach was used, in common with many other

Figure 11. Manygates School opening ceremony, 1928. *C Brooke.*

early council estates in England. The curving streets, large gardens and play areas gave Portobello a 'village' atmosphere, quite different from the grid-iron terrace streets or dark yards. It was built for a specific reason - to clear some of the slum areas in Wakefield and house the residents in new, modern council-built houses. To families moving into these houses, it must have seemed like paradise compared to their old, cramped, decaying dwellings. Wakefield Corporation, after many problems, had succeeded admirably with their task.

Sources

Primary

Wakefield Corporation Housing and Town Planning Committee Minutes November 1920 - October 1923 (West Yorkshire Archive Service ref. WWC 30/2-3).

Architects' plans for proposed houses at Portobello c.1920s (West Yorkshire Archive Service ref. C861).

West Riding Registry of Deeds, sale of land at Portobello 1924 (West Yorkshire Archive Service ref. Vol.85 402/133).

Ordnance Survey map of Portobello - 25 inch, 1933 edition (West Yorkshire Archive Service ref. 248/11).

Map of Sandal c.1800 (Wakefield Historical Society).

Large-scale maps of Kirkgate 1890 - re-drawn 1988 (Wakefield Metropolitan District Council).

Wakefield Corporation Abstract of Accounts - year ending 31 March 1925 (collection of Mr Anthony Petyt).

Oral evidence of the late Mrs Phyllis Bell.

Secondary

S Merrett, *State Housing in Britain* (1979).

C Pooley, *Local Authority Housing* (1996).

J Goodchild, 'Slum clearance and municipal housing in Wakefield: a preliminary note', *Wakefield Historical Society Journal*, Vol. 11, (1998).

M Ingham and B Andrassy, *Sandal Magna-A Yorkshire Parish and its People* (1978).

M Ingham and B Andrassy, *Sandal Magna - Another Look Back*, (1983).

P Haigh, *The Battle of Wakefield* 1460, (1996).

J W Walker, *Wakefield-Its History and People* (1939)

6. WAKEFIELD RIFLE VOLUNTEERS

by Anthony Dawson

AT THE END OF THE EIGHTEENTH CENTURY, during the war against republican France, patriotic middle-class men, with the support of local magnates, formed volunteer regiments to help to guard against the threat of invasion. In Wakefield several units were created, the most notable being the Royal Wakefield Volunteers, raised in 1794, with a strength of some 500 men under the command of Colonel John Tottenham and William Rooks Leedes Sergeantson. In 1813 this regiment was disbanded and with it went the ideas and spirit of the true volunteer part-time soldier for the next forty or so years.[1]

By the mid nineteenth century, however, there was a new wave of patriotic fervour. Again the middle-class were forming armed associations with the backing of local landowners and magnates. The move had been prompted when in May 1847 the ageing Arthur Wellesley, Duke of Wellington, told Parliament that Britain's defences were woefully inadequate. This, together with the turmoil in Europe, with revolutions in Austria, Italy, Germany and more importantly France, led to a number of MPs pressing the government for action. But nothing was done until 1859 when there was renewed fear of an invasion by Napoleon III. A mass meeting in St. Martin's Hall, London, in April of that year protested against the country's lack of defence.[2] A month later General Peel, the Secretary of State for War, sanctioned the raising of volunteer units for the internal defence of the kingdom under the terms of the 1804 *Militia Act*. By the autumn some 60,000 men had enrolled in volunteer units; two years later the figure reached 170,000.[3]

A public meeting was called in the Court House in Wood Street, Wakefield, on 6 June 1959 with the mayor presiding. It was resolved that:

> *in the likelihood there is that the present war will be of greater magnitude and duration, it is of the opinion that the formation of Volunteer Corps throughout the country with a view to the permanent training of youth in the exercise of arms, is a step that the existing circumstances render imperatively necessary …(and) that it is desirable that a Rifle Corps for Wakefield and the vicinity be forthwith established.*[4]

Figure 1. South Parade as it was in Captain Binstead's day

The committee that was formed on the occasion included George W Alder, H M Carter, J C D Charlesworth, F Dykes, Guy Fernandes, J L Fernandes jnr, D L T Foljambe, T H Holdsworth, J H Holdsworth, Edward A Mackie, E Sanderson and F Thompson. Captain C H Binstead was appointed as secretary. By 1870 Binstead attained the rank of Admiral in the Royal Navy and in that year he rented a fine town house in South Parade, Wakefield, from Mr Fernandes (Figure 1).[5] He lived there until his death in 1875.

Volunteers were to be invited to enrol and once sufficient numbers had done so a general meeting was to be called at which the officers would be elected. A subscription list was opened and the mayor was asked to inform the Lord Lieutenant of the county that a Corps was being formed.

However there was some opposition to the scheme. The *Wakefield Express* of 10 June carried a short satirical piece calling the volunteers the *Wakefield Rifle Noddle Corps* (Figure 2). The *Express*, however, was a liberal paper politically and was promoted by some of the nonconformist congregation of Zion Chapel, George Street. The attack on the mainly Tory and Church of England followers of the Rifle Volunteer movement was not, perhaps, an unexpected outburst. The *Wakefield Journal* of the same date contained a letter suggesting that the Riflemen were there to support what would today be termed the ego trips of some of the gentlemen of the town. However by 27

June the *Journal* published an article in support of the volunteers noting that thirty-two men had already enrolled and that drilling had commenced.

A month later the *Journal* noted that the government was to supply arms, on certain grounds, to the volunteers. In the same paper there is an advertisement by G W Alder, secretary to the committee, asking for volunteers and saying that prospective recruits could obtain information from him at the Old Corn Exchange on any day between 11am and 3pm. There was a further advertisement for tenders for the making up of uniforms from cloth supplied by the corps.[6] On 2 September there was an advertisement in the *Wakefield Journal* from Middleton and Glover informing volunteers that they had a 'new stock of flannel shirts, as per regulation'.

VOLUNTEER (HE OF THE 'TASTEY' UNIFORM). *"And it's so comfortable and easy, that I shall most decidedly 'shoot' in it next Season."*

Figure 2. Cartoon from Punch, February 1860, expressing some of the doubts that existed at the time in the Army and amongst the public alike over the volunteers.

Subscription lists were published in the *Wakefield Journal* on 23 September. The mayor subscribed £20. J C D Charlesworth and Joseph Barker each subscribed £25. Further sums came from J H Holdsworth (£20) and E A Mackie (£5). By then, it was reported, there were 'upwards of 70' volunteers.

Queen Victoria accepted the corps into her volunteer army on 29 November 1859 as the 9th Corps of the West Riding of Yorkshire Volunteer Rifles. The regiment was officially designated the Wakefield Rifle Volunteer Corps and was dressed and drilled as such. In 1860 the corps was renumbered the 5th, due to amalgamations in Sheffield and Bradford.[7]

Following a meeting in December 1859 three Wakefield magistrates, J C D Charlesworth, W Hepworth and T H Holdsworth, were empowered to supervise the enrolment of volunteers. A hall at the junction of Cheapside and Westgate was given over to the volunteers for drilling, as was the drill ground of the West Riding Constabulary.

Officers were appointed through a ballot system with each company voting for its own. George W Alder, was the first to be sworn in after the Lord Lieutenant had approved the formation of the corps. Captain Joseph Hulme Holdsworth, the dyer, of Belle Isle House, Portobello, was appointed commanding officer and by 1860 he had been promoted to the rank of major. Holdsworth did not, however, retain command of the regiment for long. About 1862 Edward A Mackie was appointed Captain-Commandant of the whole corps. Joseph Barker and George William Alder were appointed as the other company captains.

Joseph Barker, woolstapler and worsted spinner of Thornes, owned the mansion, Holmfield (in what is now Holmfield Park), built in 1833, which he much enlarged and modernised in 1864.[8] He served as captain-commandant from 1865-1866. It would appear that by 1866 he held the rank of major. In 1870 he became a West Riding magistrate. He was also a governor of the Wakefield Charities and a town councillor. Upon his death in 1892 his niece, Miss Secker, had the vestry enlarged in St James's Church, Thornes, in his memory; this had been built a year earlier by George W Alder. A monument was erected in the church to Barker.[9] At his death the *Wakefield Express* noted that the Major had been a conservative and a churchman and a keen follower of the Badsworth Hunt. An ornamental drinking fountain, subscribed for by his workpeople, was erected in 1893 at the entrance to Clarence Park.[10]

Each company also had a lieutenant and an ensign. Daniel B Kendall, Samuel Green, and William Thompson of Chevet Hall, all ranked as lieutenants; Robert Hart, Samuel Gurney Leatham and Frederick Thompson were appointed as ensigns. Samuel Leatham was the eldest son of John Leatham and became, with Percy Tew, a partner of the West Riding Bank.[11]

The Reverend Henry Jones was appointed as the Corps' chaplain. He was the curate at Wakefield Parish Church (now the cathedral) from November 1855 to February 1860 when he was appointed vicar of St James's Church, Thornes. He was to hold this post until 1872 when he moved to become vicar of St Mark's, Clerkenwell. He was killed accidentally on 7 May 1878.[12]

This establishment remained more or less unaltered until 1868 when William H B Tomlinson was promoted to the rank of captain to replace Captain Kendall. In 1870 Tomlinson was made a Wakefield magistrate and in 1871 he was Wakefield's mayor. Lieutenant Thompson was made a captain as was Ensign Dunn. Walter H Wright was gazetted as ensign. Captains Leatham, Barker and

Cartwright had also resigned or retired.[13] By October 1869 two more ensigns had been commissioned, James A Fawcett and a Mr Ash.

In 1876 the corps was commanded by Captain Walter H Wright who replaced Captain Thompson as Captain Commandant. Thompson had been promoted to that rank in 1869 upon the retirement of George Alder.[14] He was assisted by George Bolton who also ranked as captain. Wright was to become in 1892 the general manager and a director of the Wakefield and Barnsley Union Bank. However the same army list shows that the Corps was entitled to a major and four captains, only two of which appeared. Also there should have been four lieutenants of which only one, Francis Taylor, is shown. Frederick Whitman and William S Mackenzie both ranked as sub-lieutenant; James Fowler of 13 South Parade was appointed the Corps' assistant surgeon becoming its surgeon in 1872. The Reverend Norman Dumenil John Straton was appointed as acting chaplain replacing the Reverend Routh Tomlinson who had been chaplain from 1873 -1876. Tomlinson was a Cambridge man and was vicar of Kirkthorpe (Warmfield) from 1872 to 1882. Straton had been a curate at Market Drayton from 1865-66 and vicar of Kirkby Wharf from 1866 to 1875 and was instituted vicar of Wakefield on 2 August of that year. In 1883 he was to be made an Honorary Canon of Ripon and was the archdeacon of Huddersfield from 1888-1892. He was then consecrated as Bishop of Sodor and Man.[15]

By 1878 William S Mackenzie had been promoted to captain, and was the commander of the Normanton company. The Corps was then commanded by Lieutenant-Colonel Sheard, appointed 2 May 1877, who was aided by Majors Alex S Lee (15 May 1878) and Albany Hawke Charlesworth of Chapelthorpe Hall (2 May 1877) son of the Honorary Colonel of the regiment, John Charlesworth Dodgson Charlesworth. In 1880 J C D Charlesworth died and the rank of Honorary Colonel passed to Edward A Mackie.

At the point of creation the Corps mustered two companies, the first being formed from tradesmen and the second from clerks; the third, from working men, was added later, the plans for its formation being carried out in 1860 when vacancies were advertised in the *Wakefield Journal* on 12 October.

On 16 December 1859 an advertisement appeared in the *Wakefield Journal*:

> *Artisans and others of unexceptional character, desirous to enrol themselves can do so by paying the expenses of outfitting and annual subscription by paying weekly.*

Gentlemen of more affluence could become honorary members by paying £10 (or more) to the unit funds or paying £2 2s annually. Honorary members were allowed to drill and, like the rest of the corps, were subject to military law.[16]

On 17 June 1859 the Corps mustered 32 members but by 21 September 1860 this number had risen to 160. In 1865 each company consisted of some 60 riflemen, 4 sergeants and 2 or 3 officers (a captain and one or two lieutenants).[17] Overall command was by the senior of the captains, known as the captain-commandant in accordance with *Article 42* of the 1861 regulation and *Article* 46 of the 1863 regulations. The Corps was also entitled to an assistant surgeon or medical officer.[18] To be eligible for enrolment members had to be more than 5 feet 6 inches tall and have a 32-inch chest or more, as well as to be able to afford their uniform (£5 5s) and the annual subscription (£1 5s).

Something of the uniform is illustrated in a photograph of Corporal John Vickermann (Figure 3). Members wore a dark grey jacket faced with red and with green shoulder knots, which reached to the mid thigh and was fastened down the front by a row of eight large pewter buttons. Loose trousers, the same colour as the jacket, were worn, with a dark green welt, and black boots. Their headdress was a black shako with a silver bugle horn and crown badge and a green pompom plume. Officers wore a similar uniform but with silvered buttons bearing 3rd Admin Battalion in a garter surrounding a strung bugle horn. The front of their tunic was decorated with five lines of dark green 'frogging' à la Hussard, closing with wooden toggles. They had silvered shako fittings and a straight sword and sabretasche carried from slings from the waistbelt. In about 1876 a new scarlet tunic was adopted, reaching again to mid thigh, with dark blue facings, white cuff knots and red shoulder straps. It closed in front with eight buttons. The blue trousers had a scarlet welt. Officers wore a similar uniform though with silvered buttons, silver shoulder knots and elaborate cuff knots. In full dress silver stripes were worn to the trousers together with a red Moroccan leather shoulder belt, sword belt and slings covered with silver lace.

By 1866 the corps mustered around 270

Figure 3. Corporal John Vickermann.
Courtesy of the Castle Museum, York.

members but by 1867 it had fallen to 241 privates (riflemen) and corporals, 6 buglers, 13 sergeants and 11 officers. There was also a staff of an adjutant, a sergeant-major and a sergeant-instructor.[19] By December 1867 the corps mustered a total of 464 members; 289 were 'efficients', that is they knew their drill and were uniformed and armed; 68 were 'non-efficients', that is men still under training, and 107 were 'supernumeries', that is honorary members who did not drill.[20] In 1868 it was decided to augment the corps to a strength of four companies as the three existing companies had exceeded the regulation strength. By 1868 the numbers stood at 250, including all ranks, and by 1896 there were 313. The fourth company was removed in 1870 when membership had fallen but was revived c1874 bringing the establishment up to that of the 1860s. A sergeant-instructor who acted as sergeant-major was allowed. By 1876 the corps, with its four companies, was eligible to be commanded by a major and was considered a 'division'.

The officers' mess was in Major Barker's house, Holmfield.

As regards to higher organisation, the 'rural' companies were brought together for ease of administration into administrative battalions, in which all of the officers of each of the rural companies were compelled to serve. The Wakefield corps was grouped into an administrative battalion which ranked as third in the West Riding and which included the 28th Goole, 29th Dewsbury, 30th Birstal, 37th Barnsley and 38th Selby corps. The Selby corps was transferred out in 1863. The 37th Barnsley was attached only temporarily to the third battalion, from March 1862 to April 1863.[21] In 1867-1868 the Dewsbury Corps came up to battalion strength and therefore became independent of the 3rd Administative Battalion. In 1874 however the Dewsbury Corps transferred back in, no longer having sufficient strength to remain independent. By 1873 the Birstal Corps was disbanded. In 1867 the 43rd, or Batley Corps, was raised and added to the battalion.

The 3rd Administrative Battalion also mustered a permanent staff, who were paid, and were based in Wakefield so that the battalion was also known as the Wakefield battalion. In 1861 the staff comprised Joseph H Holdsworth as Lieutenant Colonel with William Edward Newall, late captain of the 8th Regiment of Foot, as the Adjutant and

Figure 4. Major Townley

Reverend Henry Jones as chaplain.[22]

In 1869 Major Edward Mackie of the Wakefield Corps was posted to the staff of the 3rd Administrative Battalion with the rank of Lieutenant Colonel on the retirement of Lieutenant Colonel Holdsworth.[23] Adjutant Newall died suddenly on the morning of 30 August 1870 and was replaced by Captain Richard Townley (Figure 4).[24]

With regards to drill, it was envisaged that if invasion occurred the Volunteers would act as riflemen as well as skirmishers or guerrillas. In the *Times* of 24 May 1859 Sir Charles Napier wrote with regard to the role of the Volunteers:

> *Get some old soldier for your adjutant to teach you, not a long course of drill but just seven things, viz:*
>
> *1. To face right and left at the word of command.*
> *2. To march in line and column.*
> *3. To extend in close files as light infantry support.*
> *4. To change front in extended and close order.*
> *5. To relieve the skirmishers.*
> *6. To form 'solid squares' and 'rallying squares'.*
> *7. To form and advance guard.*
>
> *These seven things are all you require. Do not let anyone persuade you to learn more.*

Sir Charles also advised,

> *Let your target practice be constant and habituate your corps to long marches of from fifteen to twenty miles, with arms and ammunition, and also to running, or "double quick" time* (Figure 5).

Drilling and the exercise and care of arms were evidently considered to be vitally important by the corps and drill musters were held every Monday and Friday evening from 7.00pm to 9.00pm at the Drill Hall and the parade ground of the West Riding Constabulary. The *Wakefield Journal* of 23 November 1860 sets out the routine for drilling:

> *No 1 Company, Thursdays, 7pm*
> *No 2 Company, Tuesdays, 7pm*
> *No 3 Company, Mondays, Wednesdays and Saturdays, 7.15pm*
> *Recruits, Mondays, Wednesdays and Saturdays, 7.15pm*
> *Bayonet drill for 1 and 2 Companies, Fridays, 7pm.*

On 15 September 1860 the entire 3rd Administrative Battalion mustered and paraded at the Wakefield Drill Room at 12.30pm before taking a train to Bradford for a grand review of Volunteers in Peel Park. The entire travel costs, it was reported, were financed by Major Holdsworth.[26] On Friday 26 September the corps went to York for a review of Volunteers at the Knavesmire where they formed part of the 1,900 strong 2nd Brigade as the 3rd Admin Battalion (Wakefield).[27] Nearly 5,000 men of the Yorkshire Rifle Volunteer Corps were present where they were reviewed by Lieutenant Colonel George Wetherall, KCB, KH before 40,000 to 50,000 spectators. The refreshments for the Volunteers were paid for by the Lords Lieutenant of each of the three Ridings. The officers of the Wakefield Corps were present at a grand military banquet at York Guildhall in the evening.[28] It was reported that Colonel Smyth, in charge of the division of which the 3rd Battalion formed a part, was 'especially pleased with the Wakefield Corps' and, while watching them execute a wheel and other drill, was heard to exclaim, 'There, that was beautifully done'.[29]

DRILL AND RIFLE INSTRUCTION

FOR THE

CORPS OF RIFLE VOLUNTEERS,

By Authority

OF

THE SECRETARY OF STATE FOR WAR.

FOURTH EDITION.

LONDON:
PRINTED BY GEORGE E. EYRE AND WILLIAM SPOTTISWOODE, PRINTERS TO THE QUEEN'S MOST EXCELLENT MAJESTY, FOR HER MAJESTY'S STATIONERY OFFICE.

PUBLISHED BY
W. CLOWES AND SONS, 14, CHARING CROSS, S.W.

1859

Figure 5. Title page of the 'Little Green Book' or the drill manual and statutes of the Rifle Volunteers.

War Office regulations were published in 1861 for the training and dress of each of the corps, as well as for their conduct. As one of the main objects of the volunteer movement was to train men in the use of rifles, and as members were keen on displaying marks of distinction, proficiency badges were authorised in 1861.

The local newspapers report many battalion events. In August 1865, for example, the Wakefield, Dewsbury and Birstal Corps held a Battalion Field Day on the Ings but the weather was poor and only 150 men appeared for the muster. The annual inspection of the battalion was announced at the time for 2 September, on Heath Common, a traditional drill ground for Wakefield troops.[30] The inspecting officer was Lieutenant Colonel Wombwell. 209 of the Wakefield Corps were present, 6 were absent with leave and 23 absent without it. Also present were the Dewsbury Corps (3 companies, 150 men), the Goole Corps (1 company, 49 men), and the Birstal Corps (1 company, 59 men). [31] At the Heath Common Field Day on 5 July 1867, when corps from Birstal, Dewsbury and Goole as well as Wakefield were again present, the battalion mustered exactly 700 men, 250 more than in 1866. [32]

Many members of the Wakefield Corps were also members of the Wakefield Enfield Rifles Club and it seems that some of these were treating the Volunteers as a uniformed gun club and did not attend drill musters. A notice appeared in the *Wakefield Free Press* of 15 August 1874 reminding volunteers that drill promoted the efficiency of individuals and of the collective and that without proficiency in drill the corps would be at a disadvantage.

In 1875 several members of the corps were fined for not achieving efficiency. They were Nathaniel Binns, Samuel Brown, Andrew Holstead, Amos Hudson, William Kershaw and Joseph Sykes; they were all of the working class, being plasterers, bricklayers etc. The case was brought by Sergeant Major Hart and they were each fined 30s (150p) plus costs.

In 1865 it was decided that the volunteers needed a permanent place to drill instead of the Constabulary depot and the National School rooms at St John's. They also needed a less mobile Orderly room than the one in Thompson's Yard or the Corn Exchange, as well as an armoury. Tenders were advertised in February for a drill shed to be built in Bank Street. [33] It seems that a trust was set up to acquire the land, known as Fair Fields. Those acting for the Volunteers were G W Alder, J Barker, W H Bedford, Robert Hart, D B Kendall, S G Leatham, E A Mackie. Work had begun by March by the following contractors: John Lockwood (bricklayer, £595 15s), W M Hodgson (carpenter, £520), William Craven (plumber, £130), C Driver (plasterer, £43 18s), J and J Hill (slaters, £125), and W Hodgson and Son (painters, £35). [34] In 1866 the West Riding Directory noted that the new drill shed was to cost £3,000, which had been raised by subscription. The shed was to have a drill room, armoury, orderly room and sergeant's quarters (Figures 6-8). There was also to be a drill ground. These arrangements for a headquarter's depot accorded with *Article 267* of the *Rifle Volunteer Statutes*. In June 1874 an emergency meeting of the officers of the corps was held to ascertain the number of trustees still available and to agree to sell the surplus land.

By 1867 it was noted that the Wakefield Corps needed a permanent range for shooting, the drill shed not being so equipped. The Corps usually used the practice ground at Pontefract, also used by the Militia. It was believed that if the Corps did have its own range

Figure 6. Wakefield Drill Hall, 1999. *Kate Taylor*

it would attract more recruits.[35]

On 30 July 1870 there was a grand review of all the Rifle Volunteer Corps in the West Riding at Heath Common when nearly 3,000 volunteers were present.[36] These included 'H' or the Wakefield Troop of the 1st West Yorkshire Yeomanry Cavalry with 49 men under Captain Taylor, and the Wakefield Rifles with 434 men under Lieutenant-Colonel Mackie. The reviewing officer was Colonel Anderson of the 22nd Foot Regiment. The event had been the brainchild of Captain and Adjutant Newall of the Wakefield Corps and 3rd Admin Battalion and his sudden death, aged only thirty-six, somewhat marred it.[37] Some 15,000 to 20,000 spectators were present and lines of carriages blocked the road to Wakefield. Proceedings began at 5.00pm following a display by the various Battalions' bands. After displays of drill and a march past in open and closed column, the different corps took up their positions for a mock battle to be held in the afternoon. The Dewsbury Corps took post on the extreme left flank and the 2nd Huddersfield were on the right flank. The Wakefield Corps took up post at the Agbrigg Bar House, with Leeds and the 1st Huddersfield in close support. The Bradford Corps was held in reserve at the entrance to Crofton Road. Captain Taylor's troop of Yeomanry was held in the rear. Colonel

Figure 7. Date stone of 1865 Wakefield Drill Hall. Above the date is carved 5th WYRV (West Yorkshire Rifle Volunteers), 1999. *Kate Taylor*

Figure 8. Drill hall interior, 1999. *Kate Taylor*

Anderson had personal command of the left flank, aided by Lieutenant Colonel Mackie and Major Robinson. The 'enemy', men of the 22nd Foot, held the high ground and were meant to be dislodged by the volunteers. The 'battle' commenced with the various corps sending out skirmishers in front of the line 'like so many swarms of bees'.[39] This was followed by the entire line advancing with a sharp fusillade, Gradually the Huddersfield and Dewsbury Corps ascended the slope, forcing back the defenders with the bayonet. The 'enemy' lost the hill but then launched a vicious counter-attack which caused the Bradford Corps to double up to give support. At the same time the Leeds Corps moved off to the left to cut of the *enemy's* escape, and sheltered behind the houses at Heath. The Wakefield Corps then advanced to support the Dewsbury Corps and drove the 'enemy' from the field. The coup de grace was a dashing charge of cavalry which brought complete victory to the volunteers. Whilst the bands took over, the volunteers enjoyed refreshments paid for by subscription by the people of Wakefield and supplied by M R Sweety of the *Bull Hotel*. Colonel Anderson then addressed the commanding officers. He noted that there was a lack of attention to bugle calls and a lack of inter-officer communication, but said that he 'couldn't expect them to be perfect' as the regulars themselves were not.

The week-long annual camp took place under canvas, with eight men to a tent, in the late summer and was normally held at Scarborough although the camps in 1871, 1873 and 1874 were at Morecambe.[39] However there was a fatality at the 1874 camp when twenty-year old Private Rowland Todd fell ill whilst at Morecambe and died of 'congestion of the brain'. He was buried in Wakefield Cemetery with military honours.

Volunteers were issued with camp rations paid for by the government but supplied via local tenders. In 1874 each man had a daily ration of 1.5 lbs bread, 1lb fresh meat, 3 oz coffee, 6 oz tea, 2 oz sugar, ½ oz salt and 39 oz pepper. The *Wakefield Free Press* suggested that the camp would be a novel experience for some of the men in having to cook their own food and make their own beds. Whilst in camp the men went through company, battalion and brigade drill and underwent inspection on the final day. The chaplain, Reverend Routh Tomlinson, conducted services using a harmonium which he had taken and the two bands.

The volunteers were presented with a silver bugle provided by the 'Ladies of the town of Wakefield' at a ceremony in the grounds of the Grammar School on 20 June 1860.[40] Mrs J C D Charlesworth of Hatfeild Hall presented it after which the corps marched past in review order. A lunch at the Corn Exchange followed with gallery tickets available at 2s 6d (12.5p) from Sergeant-Major Alder,[41]

Annual marksmanship and rifle proficiency competitions were among the highlights of the corps' activities. The first was on 3 December 1860 when competitors were given 16 rounds of ball ammunition and had to shoot 5 rounds at 150, 200 and 300 yards respectively. The prizes for those with the highest number of points were two silver cups provided by Major Holdsworth valued at £10 and £5.[42] The prize meeting in 1963 was held on 5 and 6 October at Portobello House. Members competed for prizes ranging from £25 to £5 and for an Enfield rifle and - a consolation prize - a sack of flour.[43] On 22 May 1880 a prize shoot was held at the Hartley Bank range, Dewsbury, under the supervision of the Battalion's adjutant, Major R Townley, to selected marksmen to represent the 3rd Admin Battalion in London. The four chosen were Private J Y Walker (Wakefield, 75 points), Colour-Sergeant E Wilson (Ossett, 75 points), Private S Goodyear (Wakefield, 68 points) and Corporal F Tenney (Goole, 68 points).[44]

Throughout their existence the Wakefield Volunteer Rifles hosted many social activities, mainly balls and concerts. The first was a grand concert in the Corn Exchange in aid of the band of the 3rd Admin Battalion, to which the Wakefield corps belonged, on 12 November 1860. Volunteers were expected to attend in uniform.[45] The non-commissioned officers obtained an extensive list of local patrons for a ball they hosted in the Corn Exchange on 4 January 1867. Dancing began at 9.00pm. Double tickets were 10s 6d. Members of the corps were to be in full dress.[46] By 1878 balls had become an annual event, held in the Corn Exchange in either December or January, and had been combined with the prize-giving. An unusual prize was awarded at the ball on 20 December 1878 when Mrs Green presented the awards. It was a wedding ring, donated by the Wakefield jeweller, Loveday, to be awarded to the bachelor achieving the highest number of points in contests 1, 2 and 3. If not put to its proper use it was to be forfeited before the next annual competition so that it could be competed for by volunteers more anxious to put it to its proper use! It was won by Private C Hemsworth.[47] The volunteers held a three-day bazaar in the Corn Exchange in January 1864 to raise funds for the corps and for the battalion band. Patrons included Rt Hon Lord and Lady Hawke, the Countess and Earl Fitzwilliam (the Lord Lieutenant of the West Riding), the Hon Mrs Smyth, Colonel Hormer (inspector of volunteers), and Lieutenant-Colonel J Holdsworth.

On 1 June 1880, the 3rd Administrative Battalion was converted into a 'consolidated battalion'.[48] This effectively put an end to the semi-independent existence of each corps and forged them into a single entity, with the old corps no longer operating with its own staff but now forming a company, or division of companies, within the battalion which was known as the 5th Yorkshire West Riding Volunteer Corps. The new organisation was:

A to D companies at Wakefield	*late 5th corps*
E company at Goole	*late 28th corps*
F to H companies at Dewsbury	*late 29th corps*
J and K companies at Batley	*late 43rd corps*[49]

This change was styled the 'coming of age' of the Wakefield Rifles. The celebrations took place at the same time as their twenty-first

Figure 9. Commemorative photograph of an officer group of the Wakefield Rifles in 1880. Shown with the officers are the colours of the Royal Wakefield Volunteers of 1794 which were carried at the Queen's birthday on 6 June 1880. The officers and NCOs are wearing the second, red, uniform ordered for the Corps in 1874. *Author's collection*

anniversary and Queen Victoria's birthday (Figure 9). There were great doings at Heath on 29 May when it was noted that this review would probably be the last performed by the Wakefield corps as an independent unit. Perhaps the most interesting feature of the occasion was the arrival of the colours of the Royal Wakefield Volunteers of 1796, organised by Captain Taylor of the H, or Wakefield, Troop of West Yorkshire Yeomanry who arranged that they should be taken to Heath under escort and treated with the respect that British Army colours deserved, not matter what their age (Figure 10). The colour party comprised Lieutenants Beverly and Taylor (who carried the colours) and Colour Sergeant France, Sergeant Hart, and Corporals Harrop and Goodyear who were the escort. The *Wakefield Free Press* described the presence of the colours as very evocative since both the Royal Wakefield Volunteers and the Wakefield Volunteer Rifles had been formed to guard against a possible invasion by the French under Napoleon I or Napoleon III, and that they had both lasted for a similar time span, around twenty years.[50]

Wakefield was the last of the Yorkshire Corps to be consolidated from independent units. On 5 January 1883 the announcement was made that:

> *Her Majesty has been graciously pleased to approve of the 5th York (West Riding) Regiment Rifle Volunteers being in future designated the 1st Volunteer Battalion of the King's Own Light Infantry (South Yorkshire Regiment.*

Figure 10. Major Frederick Taylor. *The John Goodchild Collection.*

The officers and men were congratulated by the Honorary Colonel, Colonel Mackie, and the Commanding Officer, Lieutenant-Colonel Sheard, on being officially associated with the 'distinguished' territorial regiment. The change in status, he remarked, did not change the service conditions of any of the members. The conversion marked the end of the Rifle Volunteer movement in Wakefield. By 1887 no Rifle Volunteer Battalions remained. The rifles hue died hard, however, with such units as the Leeds Rifles retaining their name and uniforms when they were disbanded to form the Volunteer Battalion of the Prince of Wales'

Own Regiment of Yorkshire, a title that survives to this day.

As the 1st Volunteer Battalion of the KOYLI, several organisational changes took place. By 1908 companies were located as follows: Wakefield (3 companies), Normanton(1), Goole (1), Dewsbury (2), Ossett (1), and Batley (2). In 1909 the Battalion became part of the territorial army as the 4th Battalion, KOYLI.

The Wakefield Rifles, however, also survive in the tenuous form of the 8th Battalion of the Yorkshire Yeomanry, an amalgam of the other territorial units in the district.

Notes and References

1. Cresswell family archives. See also J W Walker, *Wakefield, Its History and Its People*, 1939, pp 490-492.
2. R P Berry, *History of the Volunteer Infantry*, 1903.
3. Wyatt, p20.
4. *Wakefield Journal*, 10 June 1959.
5. Cresswell family archives. The house is the home of the present writer.
6. *Wakefield Journal*, 29 July 1859.
7. Dixon Pickup, *The West Yorkshire Rifle Volunteers 1859-1887*, 1977.
8. Kate Taylor (ed), *Wakefield District Heritage* (1976), pp138-9.
9. J W Walker, *op cit*, p306.
10. Kate Taylor, *op cit*, p144-5.
11. Walker, *op cit*, p 538.
12. *Ibid*, p306.
13. *Wakefield Journal*, 31 July 1868.
14. *Wakefield Journal*, 3 November 1869.
15 Walker, *op cit*, pp287-8.
16. *Wakefield Journal*, 16 December 1959.
17. *Wakefield Journal*, 8 September 1865.
18. R P Berry, *op cit*.
19. *Wakefield Journal*, 9 August 1867.
20. *Ibid*, 20 December 1867.
21. Dixon Pickup, *op cit*, p37.
22. Information supplied by the Prince of Wales' Own Regiment of Yorkshire.
23. *Wakefield Journal*, 10 September 1869.
24. *Ibid*, 5 August 1870.
25. Cousins, p109
26. *Wakefield Journal*, 14 September 1860.
27. *Ibid*, 21 September 1860.
28. Dixon Pickup, *op cit*, p5
29. *Wakefield Journal*, 5 October 1860.
30. *Ibid*, 18 August 1865.
31. *Ibid*, 8 September 1865.
32. *Ibid*, 5 July 1867.
33. *Ibid*, 10 February 1865
34. *Ibid*, 3 March 1865
35. *Ibid*, 20 September 1867.
36. R P Berry, *op cit*, p459.
37. He was buried at Crofton with full military honours (*Wakefield Express*, 6 August 1870).
38. *Wakefield Journal*,
39. *Wakefield Free Press*, 30 May 1874.
40. *Wakefield Journal*, 8 June 1860.
41. *Ibid*, 15 June 1860.
42. *Ibid*, 23 November 1860.
43. *Ibid*, 18 and 25 September and 2 October 1863.
44. *Wakefield Free Press*, 20 January 1883.
45. *Wakefield Journal*, 2 and 9 November 1860.
46. *Ibid*, 14 December 1866.
47. Dance card and programme.
48. Dixon Pickup, *op cit*, p35.
49. Westlake, p168.
50. *Volunteer Gazette*, and *Wakefield Free Press*, 5 June 1880.

7. DYEING FOR WAKEFIELD: THE STORY OF THE BELLE ISLE DYEWORKS

by John Goodchild

THE CURRENT AMBITIOUS SCHEME for the redevelopment of the waterside area of Wakefield involves a number of buildings and sites of once major economic significance, and of considerable historical interest to our own day. These include not only an erstwhile cloth-fulling mill, powered by the water of the river and which still retains its water wheel, the site of a boat-building yard and infilled dry dock, corn mills and maltings, a steam-powered corn mill of the eighteenth century, the Navigation warehouse of 1790, and the Navigation's flood lock, but the site too of one of the West Riding's largest and most successful cloth-dyeing factories, a site with both a fascinating and a significant history, which is now occupied by the bus depot and offices of the *Arriva* 'bus company (Figure 1).

The dyeing of cloth produced in the West Riding - and associated areas' cloth-producing districts - was of course an important industry ancillary to and part of the principal Wakefield area trade in the merchanting of cloth. It was to Wakefield that cloths undyed -

Figure 1. Offices of the Arriva bus company, 1999, (formerly offices of the West Riding Bus Company). *Kate Taylor.*

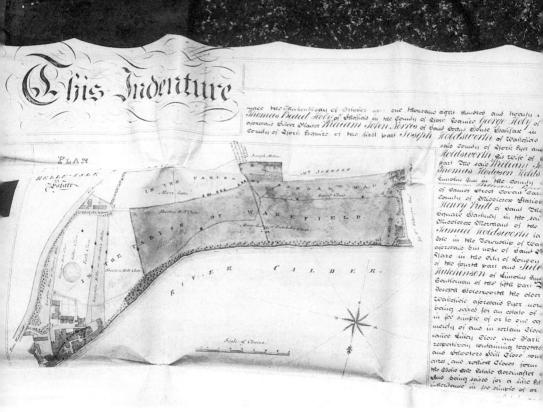

Figure 2. Part of the deed of October 1829 showing the Belle Isle estate. *The John Goodchild Collection.*

known as white cloths - were brought for surface dressing and final dyeing, before the cloths were shipped off on the Aire and Calder Navigation.

By the early eighteenth century, the Milnes family of Wakefield, whose mansions which mirrored their wealth and social standing were soon to be built in Westgate in the town, had an increasingly significant interest in the provision of cloth-dyeing facilities, and when Robert Milnes of Wakefield, cloth merchant, made his will in 1734, he referred in it to a 'house and Dyehouse with the appurtenances which I lately built' close to the then pellucid and ample waters of the River Calder; he had purchased land by the riverside in 1717 and in 1721. His dyeworks are shown on a plan of 1740-1741. although they were relatively insignificant in size, and presumably in capacity, until the end of the eighteenth century. It was apparently in 1775-1776 that the still-small works were conveyed to Richard Lumb of Wakefield, who was able to retire to the life of a country gentleman, and by conveyances of 1781 and 1789 the dyeworks and the nearby land passed to the brothers Samuel and Joseph Holdsworth. It was at this stage that the dyeworks were later described as being but 'in the compass of a nutshell' when

Figure 3. Belle Isle Dyeworks as drawn by Henry Clarke.

transferred by the 'late prosperous Mr Lumb'. The modest size of the works is shown on the Wakefield Inclosure plan of c1794, and can be compared with the much enlarged premises shown on the subsequent plans of 1829, 1848 and so forth (Figure 2).

The dyeworks formed the most westerly or upstream part of the developments on the riverside, lying on its southern side but still within the township of Wakefield: beyond them the riverside was still occupied by fields until the mid nineteenth century (Figure 3). This situation incidentally gave them the benefit of using the river water before it received any other Wakefield pollution.

The new owners of the 1780s were, significantly, members of the Presbyterian/Unitarian congregation of Westgate Chapel at Wakefield, to which the Milnes and Lumb families, their predecessors at the dyeworks, also belonged: the congregation acted as an important economic as well as social focal centre for the area around Wakefield, and the father of the two new Holdsworth partners, Stephen Holdsworth (1705-1763) had acted as superintendent of the works during

Figure 4. Westgate Chapel, 1999. *Kate Taylor*

the building of the new (and present) Chapel in 1751-1752 (Figure 4). The Holdsworths were of some standing, and the brother-partners' mother was sister to Nathaniel Hulme, MD, FRS, FSA, a man well known in scientific circles in London.

In 1786 the brothers Holdsworth agreed with a master dyer, Joshua Woodcock, to serve them for ten years from September 1785: he was to be paid a guinea a week and helped in his bankruptcy. The Woodcocks remained at the dyeworks for many decades. But the Holdsworths were not satisfied with dyeing alone and, like many other members of the Westgate Chapel congregation, they introduced to Wakefield the new wool-processing mechanical technology of the period in the form of the first local textile mills. Ebenezer Aldred built his (Wakefield's first) mill near Westgate Common in the early 1780s, to be followed by mills at Alverthorpe and at Silcoates owned by Westgate Chapel men.

At the end of 1790, a man agreed with the Holdsworths to serve as a wool scribbler for five years for either fifteen shillings a week or by the output of the wool he slubbed, plus a guinea a year, and in 1792 a draft agreement with them was reached for a man to serve as their 'Blacksmith and Engineer at & in their scribbling Engines and Woolhouses', working their 'Carders, Scribblers & Spinners of wool' for a five-year term, being also provided with a house. In 1796, following an advertisement for 'a steady Man accustomed to make up Tammies and Shalloons' in 'A Dyehouse of Considerable Business', the Holdsworth brothers agreed to employ John Rawson of Leeds for three years at eighteen shillings a week. Their wool and cloth-processing mill at Belle Isle is first listed as operational in the West Riding Cloth Searchers' lists in 1794 (and until 1797) as 'Bel isle' Mill, and something of the relative significance of the dyeing and wool processing sections of the business there is shown by their (perhaps only partial) insurance with the Sun Fire Office in 1796: £1,935 for the dyeworks, and the woollen manufactory £750.

The venture into wool and cloth was thus relatively shortlived; the principal business was in cloth dyeing, and here the Holdsworth brothers also ventured into the actual provision of one of their principal raw materials, the dyestuff woad.

At the end of the eighteenth century, growing cloth output, coupled with a claimed monopoly in the supply of woad and its associated high price, had led to the formation of a new company for the growth, processing and sale of the plant-based blue dye. The new concern was the Yorkshire Woad Company and it was formally established in February 1800 with 36 subscribers and £100 shares, the lead in its formation being taken by Joseph Holdsworth and Co of Wakefield, who in fact headed the company's executive committee along with John Halliley of Wakefield, the Chald Lane dyer, and two master dyers each from Leeds, Halifax and Saddleworth. It is of significance to note that the great factory-masters, Wormald, Fountaine and Gott of Bean Ing Mill in Leeds were among the subscribers.

The surviving papers relating to the company contain an agreement of 1800 whereby the committee of the company appointed two men, father and son, from Watford, as managers for them in the cultivation of woad during the ensuing fourteen years at £105 a year plus a commission of £1 a ton up to 100 tons a year, and then on a descending scale to 10s a ton above 200 tons in any year, on up to 500 acres of land which the company might take in Yorkshire or Lincolnshire. Samuel Holdsworth, described in the documents as a dyer, agreed in 1800, but it is not clear whether on his own or the new company's account, for two Spalding in Lincolnshire 'Cultivators of Woad' to be employed in that work on twenty acres of land near Wakefield, and Joseph Akers of Wakefield, hitherto a timber merchant, was appointed to superintend the business as manager, going to live where the cultivators and the labourers worked, supervising them and keeping the company's accounts. He was to be paid £84 a year and the company was to sell him a share in their concern: in fact, two were conveyed to him, from the three owned by James Wright and Co, dyers of Saddleworth, in June 1802. Akers had been resident at Fellgrove near Newport Pagnell and described as a woad grower; the purchase price of his shares in the Yorkshire Woad Company was five tons of woad.

In February 1803 two plots of land in the West Fen in Lincolnshire were agreed for by the Yorkshire Woad Company, containing some eighty and a half acres and taken for three years at £4 10s (£4 50p) an acre; in March 1805 the company leased some 86 acres in West Fen for woading, as the term was used. Thomas Lang, a well-known Wakefield man, was the treasurer of the new company.

The papers of the Woad Company are sparse, and its fortunes are difficult to entangle. The new lease of 1805 would perhaps suggest prosperity, but in May 1809 the company's next papers chronologically record the establishment of the company, to be called the Yorkshire Woad Company, de novo. Now the company was of thirty shares, of which Holdsworths of Wakefield took ten, and the partnership was for six years, to grow woad in Lincolnshire. Joseph Akers, now of Ackley Bridge near Boston in Lincolnshire, was another partner in the new concern. The detailed papers extend no further than the formation of the revived company; it was still in existence in May 1813, and Joseph Holdsworth (d 1819) was partner with William Gareside, dyer of Gomersal, in purchasing extensive lands in West Fen in Skirbeck, Lincolnshire, in partnership in 1819.[1]

At the end of 1802, Holdsworths took a leading part in attempting to persuade Government against the new duties imposed upon indigo and other dyestuffs imported from the East Indies. A Mr Holdsworth took the chair at an initial meeting of interested parties at Wakefield, and ultimately a petition was presented to Parliament.

Of the original Holdsworth brothers, relatively little is known personally. Samuel, the elder, was born in 1747, married quite late in life and, retired from the business, built for himself a country mansion at Crigglestone near Wakefield, where his daily life is illustrated by many surviving papers. He died, childless, in July 1826. His younger brother, Joseph, born in 1759, had married the daughter of a Macclesfield alderman, and they had a considerable family. He died in 1819; he had ceased to subscribe to the Chapel's funds some years earlier (after 1808) as had his elder brother in the 1780s. It was Joseph's son, another Joseph (1789-1857) who succeeded to the business and who raised it perhaps to its most extensive success. The factory had its own fire-fighting engine by 1807; the firm subscribed a substantial £50 in 1804 to the anti-Napoleonic Wakefield Volunteer Fund; in 1809 they sold corn to their workmen at one third below market price; but in 1832 they dealt with strikers for higher wages by bringing in blacklegs; a man arrested on suspicion of arson at the works was cleared at the Assizes.

It was the younger Joseph who apparently enlarged the works - indeed rebuilt them largely on a new and adjacent site, additional land having been purchased over the years and ultimately an area of some thirty acres being owned. By 1827 Joseph Holdsworth junior had 'considerably enlarged' the works and built corn warehouses on the site of the earlier dyehouses and presshouses, with fourteen cottages. Two mansions were built. On his father's death in December 1819 at sixty, Joseph had inherited his interest in the dyeworks, apparently initially in partnership with his own brother, Samuel Holdsworth junior; Joseph also inherited his uncle Samuel's moiety of the premises of the dyeworks. He was married in 1822 to Eliza Holy of Highfield near Sheffield, from whose family a small Sheffield estate ultimately came to the Holdsworths. Mrs Holdsworth was of Wesleyan Methodist parents and in the later 1830s she joined the congregation of West Parade Chapel, where her funeral sermon, which was printed, was preached in 1846.

In the 1820s Joseph Holdsworth experienced major financial difficulties, apparently occasioned by a number of factors. First, the great depression of 1825-26 was mirrored in Wakefield by the failure of one of the town's two banks, that of Wentworth, Chaloner and Rishworth, in which Holdsworth had a deposit; then that failure triggered off the failure of the great Wakefield cloth-merchanting firm of J and J Naylor in 1829, for whom Holdsworth had done much work and by whom he was owed £12,765 19s 4d; thirdly his own brother and partner had retired from the business (and doubtless had to be paid out) becoming a bookseller in St Paul's Churchyard in London. Again Holdsworth had spent substantially on enlarging the house known as Belle Field for his own residence by the end of 1827 and the very large corn warehouses and maltkilns had been built on part of the dyeworks estate, adjoining upon the Calder. The former family home, Belle Isle, was occupied by his widowed mother until her death in 1832. Holdsworth was able in May 1832 to legitimately claim major losses in trade, and he borrowed heavily on mortgage of his fortunately large and valuable estates - two sums totalling £40,000 in December 1827, £3,000 in 1829, and £4,500 in 1832. A deed of October 1829 describes the dyeworks premises at that time, which had been described in 1823, as consisting of

Dyehouses, Engine Houses, Wood Houses, Drying Houses, Washhouses, Warehouses & Manufactory, Blacksmith's Shop, Millwrights Shop, Carpenters Shop, Gasworks & all other tenements,

occupied by Samuel (presumably junior) and Joseph Holdsworth. Now in 1829 the premises were categorised as containing:

New Wood House, Wool scouring place, Dye Wood House, Ware Shed, Wool Wash House, Scarlet Wet House, Pattern Dyehouse, New Wood House, Low Push House, Stock House, Scalding House, New Pattern Dye House, White Cloth Wetting Engine House, Old Press Shop, Pattern Dye House, Outhouse, Wood Shed, Counting House Boilers, Indigo Mills, Rasp House, Crab House, Black Dye House, Cloth Scouring House, Chip House, Lime House, New Press Shop, Old Woad House, Webb Drying House, Gasometer House, Scalding House, Coloured Wash House, Scarlet Dye House, Lime Shed, Gas House, Counting House, Firing Place, Stove.

In 1861 reference is made to the cotton dyehouse and to the continuing use of woad, indigo etc.

Holdsworth had built some new workmen's cottages near

Wakefield Bridge End by May 1829. References occur at this period to his goods shipped to America, to his ownership of a half share in the ship *Sarah*, and to his Calcutta bills and the East India Company. His financial situation allowed in 1830 of his buying the large dyeworks of R J S Mellin on the opposite bank of the Calder from his own Works, which he let as a large worsted-spinning mill; it brought £1,000 a year as rent in the mid 1840s.

Holdsworth managed to weather the economic storms of the late 1820s and 1830s.

In 1835 the young Princess Victoria, with her mother, was disturbed when a dyer thrust a blue-stained hand and arm into their carriage in, no doubt, an excess of zeal, as they passed the dyeworks; the royal pair were revivified at Sandal Hall, later to become the home of T H Holdsworth, the then dyeworks owner (Figure 5).

Joseph Holdsworth was able to occupy in 1831-1832 the prestigious office of Constable of Wakefield, one similar in status to that of the later mayor, and as Constable he chaired the great West Riding Reform Meeting in Wakefield in 1832, and upon Wakefield becoming a single-seat Parliamentary borough in that year, he was appointed its returning officer. This appointment came only a couple of months after his being approached by the local Tories as a prospective candidate for the representation of the borough. He was in fact a Liberal; the Reform Meeting of 1832 was said to have marked his first appearance in public life and in July 1841 he was returned as MP for Wakefield in the Liberal interest with a majority of 28 votes, but he was still nominally returning officer and hence disqualified from election as a Member, and after a Parliamentary hearing, his Tory opponent was declared elected. He was said to have been invited at the next election to stand by both parties but declined as his wife had died.

Fjigure 5. Sandal Hall, 1999. *Kate Taylor.*

Holdsworth was an active magistrate, appointed in 1832, and for some time chairman of the Wakefield bench. He was also a West Riding Deputy Lieutenant. He moved from Belle Field to the larger country mansion Belle Vue, whose parkland is now Wakefield Cemetery, in about 1842. He was elected an alderman of the newly constituted (1848) municipal borough of Wakefield, and office which he held from 1849 to 1853; in November 1849 he was elected mayor, an office which he held for the usual year. He died in April 1857. He had been in failing health for almost two years and some six weeks before his death he had gone to Leamington,

in the hope of receiving some permanent benefit from the more genial climate of that place,

where he died. He was described at his death as having been a warm and liberal supporter of various charitable and benevolent institutions, and as a magistrate as the 'zealous, efficient, courteous, and impartial chairman of this court.' At his death, Joseph Holdsworth's real estate, divided among his two sons, was valued at £22,000 in the Wakefield area and another £7,200 in Sheffield. The corn warehouses fronting the Calder brought £800 a year from four tenants, Porto Bello Worsted Mills £450 a year, while the dyehouses' tax assessments were £322 for the buildings and a further £152 for the engine, shafting, etc. Holdsworth's personal estate was valued at £68,000 (making his total fortune nearly £100,000, including:

	£	s	d
Machinery at Belle Isle Dyeworks	2,628	0	2
Portobello Worsted Mills	2,511		
Barnsley Canal shares	1,029	4	0
Manchester & Liverpool District Bank shares	4,158	5	10
Wakefield Borough Market Shares	70		
Denby Dale Road Exchequer Loan debt	289		
Ings Road debt	25		
Leeds Philosophical Hall shares	38		
And railway shares - the largest NER Berwick stock	6,709	10	0

In 1859 the works had been described as consisting of dyehouses, press shops, machinery, drying and other chambers etc. plus 4 corn warehouses, 1 mansion (Belle Field House) and 25 cottages, plus Portobello Mills, the whole being of a saleable value of some £10,800. In 1857 the machinery at the works was valued at £2,628

0 2d and at Portobello Worsted Mills £2,511. A firm had apparently agreed in 1854 to deposit goods to secure their account with Holdsworths up to £5,000 - Coburgs (a twill cloth made from cotton and silk, worsted and silk or all worsted, introduced after Victoria's marriage to Albert), Orleans (plain weave cloth with cotton warp and worsted weft), Alpaca, Circassians (a lining cloth).

By 1829 a reservoir had been built on a hill on the site, to which the river water was pumped (the hill survived as a recognisable feature into the 1960s) and there was passed through two filters before being used in the works. In 1851 the works had a 55 hp low pressure steam engine, one of the most powerful in Wakefield at that time.

In 1840 a man had been killed by accidentally falling into a pan of boiling water at the works, and from as early as 1807 the works had their own fire engine, which they continued to maintain far into the second half of the nineteenth century.

But the textile industry was changing and more and more mills had their own dyeworks, while Holdsworths' success had itself been one cause of numbers of further dyeworks being established in Wakefield. From about 1863, a part of the works was let off to Robert Dent, who had worked for Holdsworths 'on and off' for forty years and as a dyer for about seventeen. Dent employed about 100 persons when at full work, and undertook the stuff or worsted trade, while Holdsworths continued to dye woollens. Dent complained that the water of the Calder was not now as good as once it was for dyeing scarlets, crimsons and yellows. In 1863 Hodgson, Shaw and Dent of the Belle Isle Dyeworks, partners, agreed to employ a pattern dyer for five years, one William Heatherington, at £4 per week and an extra £10 a year, but found themselves soon in difficulty when he was enticed away, and a High Court suit ensued.

In 1871 it was agreed to sell a part of the Holdsworth dyeworks estate to Joseph Hopps of Apperley Bridge, dyer, at £4,300 for the land and buildings and £878 17s for the machinery and fixtures, the property including a landing stage on the banks of the Calder: Hodgson, Shaw and Dent had given up by 1870. Meanwhile, the main part of the dyeworks was run by Thomas Holy Holdsworth and his brother Joseph Hulme Holdsworth, of Portobello. The latter died at the end of 1881 aged only fifty-one and childless; he had married at forty-six the daughter of a vice-admiral; he left just over £17,000; his will is witnessed by a cook and a housemaid. T H Holdsworth seems to have given up business soon after his brother's death, and even in 1879 a part of the works had been offered for sale: he is

Figure 6. Portobello House, as drawn by Henry Clarke.

shown as a dyer in the 1887 directory, but not in that of 1888. He was to live on at Sandal Hall, which he had occupied since 1858 and bought in 1865 for £7,782 until his death in 1911 at the age of eighty-four: he took a very active part in the affairs of Wakefield and Sandal. In 1874 land, part of the Porto Bello Dyeworks estate, had been sold to George and James Stubley of Batley for the building of their new factory in Portobello Road, and land was also sold to J S Booth for an adjoining factory. Portobello House had been built in 1825-6 for a Holdsworth, and was to let in 1841 (Figure 6).

Meanwhile, perhaps as a continuation of the Hopps business, the Belle Isle Dyeing Co Ltd worked at Belle Isle (and in Bradford) for many more years, appearing on the trade directory of 1897 as of Wakefield and Bradford, but in that of 1904 as Bradford only. By deeds of 1904 T H Holdsworth conveyed land and buildings at Belle Isle to the Yorkshire Electric Tramways Construction Syndicate Ltd to form the site of their tramways' power station and tram sheds. Dyeing had died.

Sources

The information contained in this study is derived entirely from the Holdsworth manuscripts and the Wakefield newspaper index in the John Goodchild collection at Wakefield.

Note

1. Woad Farm at Skirbeck, Boston, is described as '*the last place in the world*' to grow woad as a crop. Its last crop was grown in 1932. *Transactions of the Newcomen Society, Vol 43*, 1974, pp205-206.

8. FROM FARMS TO STAGE AND SURGERY: THE WOOD FAMILY OF CRIGGLESTONE AND WEST BRETTON

by Anthony Petyt

IN NOVEMBER 1888, THE WAKEFIELD-BORN NOVELIST, George Gissing, was making a tour of Italy (Figure 1). On 20 November he stayed the night at Pompeii in preparation for a visit to Vesuvius the next day. At dinner that evening he overheard a man speaking German - but with a very familiar accent. Afterwards, he made the man's acquaintance and found he was a Yorkshireman - with a very strong Yorkshire accent. He was John Wood Shortridge, born in Barnsley but who had lived in Italy for seventeen years. His wife was from Capri and they lived at Massa Lubrense near Sorrento. He surprised Gissing further by revealing that he was related to Wakefield people whom Gissing knew well. They included Dr William Wood, the Gissing family's physician, who was Shortridge's

great uncle, and Joseph Tolson White, a mining engineer who was Shortridge's cousin. They were members of a quite remarkable family who had been farmers and maltsters in Crigglestone and West Bretton. Several descendants of this family were to become significant figures in the Wakefield area and one of them was to achieve success on a national and international scale.

In the 1750s John Wood and Margaret, his wife, took the tenancy of Blacker Hall Farm in Crigglestone (Figure 2). The hall had been owned by the Blacker family for over two hundred and fifty years, but by the time the Woods moved there, the old hall had gone and the estate was owned by the Buxton family. From John Wood's will, written in 1803 and proved in 1809, it seems that he was a general farmer, keeping livestock and growing the usual arable crops. The malting business was to develop later.

Figure 1. Wakefield-born novelist George Gissing.

Figuare 2. Blacker Hall Farm, 1998. *A Petyt.*

John and Margaret had four sons and four daughters. All the daughters, Hannah, Elizabeth, Mary and Sarah survived childhood and married. All benefited from their father's will, but maybe John was not too sure of his sons-in-law as he made provision for his daughters to control their own legacies - except for Elizabeth, wife of Lionel Garlick. Perhaps he was not too sure of her, even, because her legacy of £120 was controlled by her brother, Thomas. This arrangement was still operating in 1846 when Thomas died.

Of John Wood's four sons, Charles and John died as young adults. The two older boys, Joseph and Thomas, stayed in the Crigglestone area as farmers and maltsters. John's wife, Margaret died on 4 July 1800 and he followed her on 21 May 1809. They are buried under an impressive altar tomb in Sandal churchyard. The tenancy of Blacker Hall passed from John to his eldest son, Joseph, who had been born in 1756. Joseph married Elizabeth Sykes at Sandal church in 1776 and they had nine children. Of four sons two were named John, one dying in infancy and the other surviving his father by only a few years. The other sons were Thomas, born 1790 and Joseph, born 1803. Both succeeded in turn to the tenancy of Blacker Hall. Of the daughters, Sarah, Mary and Hannah died young. Ann married James Bramald, but of the youngest, Margaret, nothing more is known. Like his father, Joseph was a general farmer, though in his will he describes himself as a farmer and butcher. He died in 1819 and the farm was taken over by his son, Thomas.

Thomas carried on farming at Blacker Hall in the traditional manner, but like his cousins, John and Thomas Wood at West Bretton, he began the production of malt. This was a very profitable line of business and soon led to the expansion of the farm buildings. The large malting shed still stands at Blacker Hall. In 1828 Thomas married Hannah Robinson and they had a son, John and a daughter, Margaret. Thomas died in 1856 and the farm was then managed by his unmarried brother, Joseph, and Thomas's son John. Their business continued to thrive and in the 1871 census returns, Joseph is listed as a maltster and farmer of 130 acres and employing two men and two boys. Joseph was then 68 years of age and unmarried. Still living with him was his unmarried nephew, John Robinson Wood who was forty-one.

By the time of the next census in 1881, Joseph had given up the tenancy of Blacker Hall and had retired to a house on Branch Road, Crigglestone. He died on 29 May 1890, aged 83 and was buried in the family grave at Sandal. His nephew, John, gave up farming also. He married late in life and by 1881 he was the landlord of the *Lancashire and Yorkshire Hotel* on Ackton Road in Castleford. He did not follow his new occupation for long but died in 1883 and was buried in Crigglestone cemetery. On his gravestone is an inscription to the memory of his grandson, Arthur Sykes, who was killed in action in France on 1 November 1918.

Thus ended the Wood family's connection with Blacker Hall after almost 150 years. We should remember, however, that the original tenant, John Wood, had another son, Thomas who farmed at Birch Laithes, West Bretton (Figure 3). Thomas was a maltster and farmer, but he, too, was the father of an interesting family. Thomas held the tenancy of Birch Laithes Farm from the Bretton Hall Estate on a yearly basis. This agreement was to cause problems for his son, also Thomas, in later years. Thomas was a farmer and maltster, helped in his business by his sons, until they either obtained farms of their own or left to take up other pursuits. That Thomas was a very good businessman is evidenced by the fact that when he died in 1846 he left almost £4,000, a very large amount of money for those days. At the time of his death only one of his daughters was still living. This was Mary and she was left £800; she soon found a husband - or a

Figure 3. Birch Laithes Farm, West Bretton, 1998. *A Petyt.*

Figure 4. Bullcliffe Farm, West Bretton, 1998. *A Petyt.*

husband soon found her because she was married to John Nicholson within six months of her father's death. Thomas's eldest daughter, Sarah, who had married Matthew Mason at Sandal in 1825, had been dead for some years but she had a son, Thomas Mason, who received a legacy of £600. The other daughter, Hannah, born in 1815 died in the 1840s unmarried.

The four sons, John, Joseph, Thomas and William were all provided for and their careers and families will be dealt with subsequently. Thomas's wife, Martha, died in 1845 and Thomas died the following year. They are both buried with John and Margaret Wood in Sandal churchyard. Thomas's eldest son, John, was born in 1799. He received what little education he had from the curate at Chapelthorpe and by the age of twelve was working on his father's farm. It was there that he learned the skills of malting and by 1838 he was established on his own farm at Bullcliffe (Figure 4). By then he had a wife, Elizabeth, and they had two daughters, Elizabeth and Mary Ann. Besides his farming activities he held minor public positions in West Bretton being elected an Overseer of the Poor in 1848 and 1851 and a Surveyor of the Highways in 1853. His wife died in 1859 but he continued to live and farm at Bullcliffe until the late 1860s. When he retired from farming he went to live with his cousin, Joseph Wood, at Blacker Hall and died there in 1874.

Twenty years earlier in 1854, his daughter Mary Ann had become the second wife of Joseph Tolson White. White, born at Wakefield in

1821 would have been well-known to the Wood family as he had lived at Cliffe House at Crigglestone from 1827 to 1839. Tolson White almost certainly received his early education at the curate's school at Chapelthorpe but later he became one of the first pupils at the new West Riding Proprietary School in Wakefield. His father, William White, was a wine merchant with premises on Westgate in Wakefield and this business was later taken over by his son-in-law William Fennell. William's eldest daughter, Louisa, was to leave her mark in Wakefield; she was a very talented artist and painted a number of Wakefield scenes. Examples of her work may be seen in the city art gallery.

Tolson White was a Mining and Civil Engineer who specialised in drawing up plans for coal mines such as the one at Low Laithes. He did a great deal of work in Wakefield, in 1849 the Street Commissioners awarded him a contract to ventilate the town's drains and two years later he drew up a plan of the town. His business premises, along with his living accommodation, were at the top of Westgate until the site was acquired for the building of the Wakefield and Barnsley Union Bank. He then moved the office to the other side of Westgate and went to live at Halesfield, a very large house at Altofts (Figure 5). White was a keen churchman being a churchwarden at Wakefield Parish Church and at one time secretary of the Wakefield Church Institution. He served on many committees including the local 'Committee for the Great Exhibition of 1851' which included such people as Charles Waterton of Walton Hall. He was appointed a Justice of the Peace. Tolson White died in 1874 and his business was taken over by Joseph Fletcher White, his son from his first marriage. His second wife, Mary Ann Wood, survived him only by a few months and was buried with him in St. John's churchyard on 6 December 1878. Their son, William Thomas White, who was born in 1856, seems not to have inherited an enthusiasm for

Figure 5. Halesfield, Altofts, 1998. *A Petyt.*

hard work from either his father or his Wood relatives. In 1881 he was living in the *George Hotel* on Westgate, describing himself at the age of twenty four as a 'retired articled clerk'.

Thomas Wood's second son, Joseph, was born in 1801. Like his older brother, John, he attended the school at Chapelthorpe but according to his son he was also sent to two boarding schools, one at 'Sand Mill' run by a Mr Haw and another at Emley. By the age of twelve his father decided that his education was complete and he started work on the family farm. He spent the next twelve years learning the skills required of a farmer and maltster but in 1825 he decided that he wanted to see more of the world. He left home and in a letter to his father told him that he was going to London to seek his fortune. In London he found lodgings with two Yorkshire ladies and their nephew. The nephew offered to show Joseph the sights of London and one evening they visited *Drury Lane Theatre* to see a performance of *Guy Mannering*. Joseph was so impressed by the play that he decided to make the stage his career. The next day he went to see Robert Elliston, manager of *Drury Lane Theatre* but did not receive any encouragement. He went then to see Charles Kemble, manager of *Covent Garden Theatre*, who was very helpful. Kemble advised Joseph to spend the next year having his voice trained and learning the art of acting. This plan required money so Joseph wrote to his father explaining the situation. Thomas sent the necessary funds and Joseph was soon on his way to Ireland to study under a Mr Philips. He had more problems losing his Yorkshire accent than in the training of his voice, but he worked hard and within a year he made his first appearance on the stage in Dublin playing the part of Hawthorn in *Love in a Village*. In 1827 he returned to London and was engaged at *Covent Garden* as second tenor.

Joseph was a great success and won acclaim for his singing. He went on to play many leading roles both in London and the provinces (Figure 6).

Appearing with Joseph in Dublin in 1826 was a young singer, Mary Ann Paton. Mary Ann had been born in Edinburgh in 1802, the daughter of George Paton, a writing-master and amateur violinist. She, with her sisters, received a good musical education and by the age of eight had made several public appearances as a singer and performer on the harp and piano. In 1811 the Paton family moved to London where Mary Ann was to give more public performances. Not surprisingly her health broke down and she 'retired' from public life for a period of six years. By 1820 she had fully recovered and in that year she appeared as a singer at concerts in Bath. The following year she was at Huntington and in 1822 she joined the Haymarket Company and performed many operatic roles (Figure 7). About this time Mary Ann formed an attachment to a young medical man by the name of Blood. He was a surgeon at St Thomas's Hospital and claimed to be a lineal descendant of the notorious Colonel Blood who had attempted to steal the crown jewels from the Tower of London in 1671. Mr Paton refused to consent to the match and the engagement was broken. In 1824 she made the acquaintance of a man more to the liking of her father. He was Lord William Pitt Lennox, son of the Duke of Richmond and they were married on 7 May 1824. The marriage was not a success and was dissolved by the Scottish Courts in 1831. Soon after her divorce she married Joseph Wood. In the year of their marriage Joseph and Mary Ann appeared at *Drury Lane* and the following year they were at the *Royal Victoria Theatre*. In 1834 they paid their first visit to America. There

Figure 6. An engraving of 1829 with Joseph Wood as Tom Tug, and Miss Cawse as Wilhelmina in The Waterman.

they were engaged to play many parts at the *New Theatre* in New York. In 1835 they returned to America, staying for more than a year. In 1837 they were again at *Drury Lane* and gave performances at other theatres, all to great applause.

In 1840 Joseph and Mary Ann made their third and last visit to America.

In the 1830s Joseph had wisely invested their earnings in a small country estate of 120 acres at Woolley Moor in Crigglestone (Figure 8). They spent most of their time between engagements at Woolley Moor House and it was here in 1838 that their only child, Robert, was

Figure 7. An engraving of Miss Paton.

born. Having been brought up as a farmer Joseph spent a great deal of time and money in improving his property. He rebuilt the house, which is still there. It is now the Woodlands Nursing Home. They both took an interest in local charities and they trained
the choir at Chapelthorpe Church where Mary Ann often played the organ. In earlier years they had performed in Wakefield at the *Theatre Royal* and at concerts at the Corn Exchange and always to capacity audiences. In 1844 they appeared together at the *Princess's Theatre*, London but later that year they decided to retire from the professional stage and returned to their home in Yorkshire.

In 1852 Joseph had a serious accident on his farm. When at home he had always helped with the work and on this particular occasion he was helping his men thresh some wheat. It seems that he had climbed onto the threshing machine when his foot slipped and he fell into the moving parts. He was seriously injured and it was thought that he could not possibly survive. However, with expert help from his doctors, one of whom was his younger brother, William, he eventually went on to make a full recovery.

In 1854 Joseph and Mary Ann left Woolley Moor House and went to live abroad for two years. They returned to England in 1856 to live in Leeds where they set themselves up as teachers of singing. In 1863 Mary Ann's health broke down and they returned to West Bretton where they lived with Joseph's elder brother, John, until Mary Ann died on 21 July 1864. The following year Joseph married Sarah Dobson who had been one of his pupils at Leeds. Sarah had achieved some success because in 1862 she had been engaged to sing soprano roles at *Covent Garden*. After their marriage they spent a short time abroad and then settled down as singing teachers in Woodhouse Lane, Leeds. In 1872 they left Leeds for the more pleasant surroundings of Harrogate. Joseph and Sarah had a family of five

Figure 8. Woolley Moor House in 1902. The house was built by Joseph Wood in the 1830s.

children, the youngest, Alice, being born when he was seventy-nine years of age. Joseph died peacefully on 6 September 1890 in his eighty-ninth year and is buried in the old cemetery at Harrogate.

It was Thomas's third son, another Thomas, who took over the tenancy of Birch Laithes Farm. Presumably he had worked on his father's farm since leaving school and as his two older brothers were established he was given the opportunity to carry on the family business. His father had left him £400 and the right to buy all the farming stock and equipment at a fair price. In 1830 he had married Sarah Ann Mould from High Hoyland at Sandal and they had one child, a daughter, Sarah Martha born in 1834. Like his brother, John, Thomas was also elected to minor public positions. In 1848 he was a Surveyor of the Highways for Crigglestone and in 1853 was an Overseer of the Poor. In 1850 he had been a member of the Grand Jury of Intermediate Sessions at Wakefield.

In 1858 Thomas, for reasons unknown, was given notice to quit Birch Laithes Farm on 1 May 1859. This move on the part of the Bretton Hall Estate was quite legal because in 1856 Thomas had agreed to the arrangement for a yearly tenancy made by his father in 1816. Thomas disputed the wording of the notice to quit and the case went to court. Thomas made two appearances in court but to no avail. The court found in favour of the landlord and on 31 July 1859 he was given twenty one days to leave the farm. What happened to Thomas after the eviction is not known. His wife, Sarah Ann, died near York on 18 May 1875. At the time of her death she was acting as housekeeper to her unmarried brother, Thomas Mould, who was a farmer at Cuckoo Nest Farm, Low Caton. Thomas and Sarah's daughter, Sarah Martha, married Richard Shortridge at Monk Bretton Church in 1850 when she was just sixteen years of age. Richard was the son of John Shortridge, railway contractor of Sheffield, and a partner in the firm of Shortridge and Wright, gunpowder manufacturers of Worsbrough Dale, Barnsley. Richard and Sarah set up home in Barnsley and over the next thirteen years they had seven children. Both Richard and Sarah died young, Richard in 1865 and Sarah in 1867. Their children were brought up and educated by their wealthy Shortridge relatives.

The eldest child was John Wood Shortridge and the man George Gissing met in Italy in 1888. John had moved to Italy as a young man, met and married a local girl, Carmela Esposito, and fathered a family of ten children. The marriage was a very stormy one and eventually John left his wife and settled in New Zealand with his children. Living with John at the time of Gissing's visit was his younger brother, Herbert, who was studying medicine.

However, Herbert, was suffering from consumption and this combined with an alcoholic problem led to his early death in 1890 at the age of twenty-three. He was buried on the island of Capri. Of the other children, two of the daughters married well, Ellen married a naval man, Alfred Coad and Sarah married Dr Samuel Aird Jolly. The second son, Thomas, qualified as a doctor, married and settled in Devon and the youngest son, Richard, joined the Merchant Navy. The youngest of Thomas's sons was William born at Birch Laithes in 1813. He must have received a better education than his brothers because he went on to qualify as a doctor (Figure 9). By 1851 William was well established as a physician and surgeon in Wakefield with a house in Cheapside. In later years he was to move house several

Figure 9. Dr William Wood, the prison surgeon.

times finally settling in Vincent House, a large Georgian house halfway down Westgate (Figure 10). In 1858 when he applied for the post of surgeon to the West Riding House of Correction his qualifications were given as a licentiate of the Apothecaries Company, London, member of the University of Edinburgh, member of the Royal Colleges of Surgeons of Edinburgh and London and also a Fellow of the London Royal College of Surgeons. Amongst those giving testimonials were Dr Hobson, physician to the Leeds Infirmary, a one-time friend and later biographer of Charles Waterton, and William Stewart the Wakefield solicitor. William's application was successful and he was awarded the post with a salary of £225 per year. For many years he was certifying factory surgeon to the Wakefield district and he was also the medical officer for the Yorkshire district of the Lancashire and Yorkshire Railway.

Dr Wood was one of the Wakefield Street Commissioners who held their meetings in the room over the Market Cross in Cross Square and after the incorporation of the borough he sat on the town council as a Conservative councillor for the St. John's ward. He was a staunch churchman and served as churchwarden at the parish church holding the post of chairman of the churchwardens in 1851. Dr Wood was also a considerable traveller visiting Europe and

America several times during the course of his long life. William Wood was married three times. Firstly to Anne Dyson, daughter of Timothy Dyson, landlord at the *Lord Rodney Inn* on Westgate. They married in 1843 at Wakefield Parish Church and had a family of six children. Anne died in 1870 and was buried at Sandal. In April 1872 William married Christian Ingram, a sixty year old spinster living at St John's. Their happiness was to be short-lived as Christian died in September of the same year. The following year William married Hannah Pickslay at Harrogate. She was the widow of Edwin Pickslay, a Wakefield solicitor who lived on Westgate at the same time as the Woods. She was also the daughter of the late William Starkey, surgeon of Wakefield. Sadly this marriage was not to last long; Hannah died in 1878 after only five years.

William was to live for another eleven years and after retiring from his practice he lived at Sandal in Woodlands Cottage quite close to the parish church (Figure 11). It was there that he died on 9 May 1889 and in spite of his request for a quiet family funeral it was attended by most of the leading people of Wakefield. He was laid to rest with his first wife, Anne, in Sandal churchyard next to all his Wood ancestors. Four of his children survived childhood. His eldest son, William, was a doctor and at the time of his death held the post of Medical Officer of Health for the County of Oxford. John, born in 1847, was a graduate of Oxford University but it seems that he and his father had some sort of disagreement for when William died he left John 'twenty pounds in remembrance of early days'. His daughter Katherine married a Wakefield solicitor, Richard Langhorne. His youngest son was the last member of the Wood family to make a mark in Wakefield. Francis Henry Wood was born in 1853 and was a graduate of Edinburgh University. He was a general practitioner and lived at Arundel House on Northgate. Francis Wood and George Gissing were on friendly terms. Gissing mentions him in his diary and correspondence and he occasionally dined with the Woods when he visited Wakefield. Another link between the two families was

Figure 10. Vincent House, Westgate, home of Dr Wood. The house is only a short distance from the prison.

Figure 11. Woodlands Cottage, Sandal, 1998, the last home of Dr Wood.
A Petyt.

forged when Wood sent his son, Bertram, to the boys' preparatory school run by Gissing's sisters, Margaret and Ellen. For many years he was certifying surgeon under the *Factory and Workshop Acts* and he was physician at Clayton Hospital. He also was the medical referee for several insurance companies. For the last twelve years of his life he was a magistrate and at the time of his death the Mayor of Wakefield (Cllr G Blakey) made reference to the valuable work he had done on the Bench. Francis died in 1920 and his widow and son, also a doctor, left the district. Their leaving marked the end of a most remarkable family's links with Wakefield and the surrounding villages.

Sources and Bibliography.

Wakefield Express. Wakefield Journal and *West Riding Herald. Wakefield Echo. Barnsley Chronicle.*
Parish registers of All Saints, Wakefield, St. John's, Wakefield, Sandal Magna, Chapelthorpe, Bretton, High Hoyland and Monk Bretton.
Census Returns, 1841-1891.
Various Wills of the Wood and Shortridge families.
Barnsley Cemetery internment book.
Coustillas, P., *The Diary of George Gissing*, 1978.
Hewitt, J, *History and Topography of Wakefield*, 1862.
Dictionary of National Biography.
Taylor, C M P, *Right Royal—Wakefield Theatre 1776-1994*, 1994.
Turner, J Horsfall, *The Annals of the Wakefield House of Correction*, 1904.
Wainwright, K, *Crigglestone Backtrack*, vol. 3, 1995.
Walker, J W, *Wakefield, Its History and People*, 1939.
West Riding Proprietary School, Opening Proceedings, 1834.
Wood, J D, *Joseph Wood- a Biography*, 1890.

9. THE HISTORY OF WEST PARADE METHODIST CHAPEL

by Paul Dawson

METHODISM IS A CHRISTIAN DENOMINATION which originated in England with the work of John Wesley (1703-1791) in the 1730s as an evangelical movement within the Church of England. Methodists were to live their lives according to the 'Christian Method'. The movement spread rapidly through the country as Wesley toured it. It became a separate church only after his death, in 1795. Further denominations developed from it: in 1797 the Methodist New Connexion was founded by Alexander Kilman and William Thom. There were those who found the Wesleyan Methodists too middle class and who founded the Primitive Methodist Church in 1812. In 1830 criticism of the manner in which Jabez Bunting (1779-1858) led the Methodist Church nationally resulted in the founding of the Protestant Methodists. Then in 1848 James Everitt founded the Church of Wesleyan Reformers. Eleven years later this merged with the Protestant Methodists to form the United Free Methodist Church. In 1907 the Methodist New Connexion and the United Free Methodists came together as the Methodist Free Church and in 1933 the act of union brought this, the Wesleyan Methodist Church and the Primitive Methodists together as the Methodist Church.

At one time Market Street had both a Primitive Methodist Chapel,

Figure 1. Drawing of the West Parade scheme. *Courtesy of Wakefield Museum.*

Figure 2. West Parade from South Parade, in the 1870s.

built in 1838 and rebuilt in 1880, and a chapel of the United Methodist Free Church, built in 1858. The Methodist New Connexion chapel was opened in Grove Road on 15 February 1866. A United Free chapel (Brunswick) was built in Savile Street in 1876. But West Parade was always Wakefield's most prestigious Methodist chapel and its congregation has included many of the city's leading inhabitants (Figures 1 and 2).

The founder of the Methodist movement in Wakefield was Francis Scott, a joiner and cabinet maker who had a shop in Scott's Yard. When John Wesley first came to the town, on 25 November 1743, he noted:

> *at the desire of Arthur Bate, I rode to Wakefield; but I soon found I had not come to talk but to listen.*

Five years later, on 20 August 1748, he wrote:

> *At the earnest desire of the little society I went to Wakefield. I knew the madness of the people there, but I knew also they were in God's hands. At 8.0 I would have preached in Francis Scott's yard but the landlord would not suffer it, saying the mob would do more hurt to his house than ever we should do him good; so I went perforce into the main street (Westgate) and proclaimed pardon for sinners. None interrupted or made the least disturbance from beginning to end.*

On one of his further visits to Wakefield, in 1751, Wesley was brought before the magistrates, at the *White Hart Inn*, for preaching in the streets, but only a year later, on 12 April 1752, he preached in the parish church. His visit on 30 August 1773 was, however, to lay the foundation stone of the Methodist Society's own meeting house in Thornhill Street.

For this Francis Scott had bought 338 yards of land in Thornhill Street from Edward Popplewell. The building itself cost £500, financed by subscriptions and loans, the latter including one of £250 from James Milnes. The meeting house was opened by Wesley on 28 April 1774.

Income towards paying off the debt came from the rent for seats, collections and classes. In 1799 rents for the front seats were fixed at 5s 6d per half year and for the corner pews at 2s 6d. Francis Scott was the chapel treasurer. Between 1786 and 1788 the trustees built a manse and in 1795 they built a further preacher's house, borrowing money for each.

The growth of the congregation was such as to warrant the building of a new larger chapel to hold 1,500, with room for a Sunday school, by 1801. This was to be West Parade. The site was bought from George Charnock for £537 and lay close to Charnock's housing scheme for South Parade, designed by the Doncaster practice of Charles Watson and William Lindley. The chapel itself was in a neo-classical style in red brick. The surviving accounts show that tradesmen involved in the work were also subscribers to the building fund. They included:

Tradesman	Trade	Account	Subscription
John Robinson	*bricklayer*	£1,030 2s 0d	£50
William Scott	*joiner*	£713 3s 0d	£50
Benjamin Saville	*mason*	£129 9s 6d	£5
John Newhouse	*plumber/glazier*	£153 19s 6d	£50
Stephen Hargett	*carpenter*	£661 9s 1d	£30

The total outlay was £3,842 2s 5d. Once West Parade was opened the earlier meeting house was closed and was sold to the Quakers for £500. It remained in use by the Society of Friends until 1965 when it was replaced by the present building on the same site (Figure 3).

The first trustees were William Bircliffe, John Crowther, Robert Drake, Richard Earnshaw, John Gaulter, John Gregory, Thomas Hadfield, Stephen Hargett, John Hartley, Joseph Holdsworth, Abraham Lee, John Kempe, Benjamin Kitson, Thomas Laycock,

Figure 3. The Friends Meeting House, Thornhill Street, 1999. *Kate Taylor*

John Lee, John Newhouse, Joseph Scott, Joseph Scott jnr, Thomas South, William Spicer, John Tootal, John Walton, William Walton, Thomas Williams and John Wood.

A manse was built in West Parade close to the chapel (Figure 4)

Much of the chapel income came from pew rents. In September 1804 it had 286 sittings on the ground floor, bringing in £36 16s 6d a half year and 461 gallery seats bringing in £61 3s 4d, making a half yearly income of £97 19s 10d. Rents were raised in January 1808. The gallery front seats were set at 2s 6d (12.5p) per half year, the second row at 2s (10p), the fourth and fifth at 1s 6d and the remainder at 1s. Downstairs seats in the eight rows at the rear of the

Figure 4. West Parade manse, taken from the Methodist Recorder of 1900. *From the collection of Paul Dawson*

chapel were 1s 6d (7.5p) per annum, those in the other side pews were 2s 6d (12.5p) and in the pews in the main body of the chapel were, depending on their position, 1s 6d (7.5p) or 2s (10p). By 1813 the annual income from pew rents was £300 and had been rising steadily since 1810. Nevertheless the chapel history is one of endless fund-raising, borrowing, and servicing debts.

The Sunday school, held for many years in rooms underneath the chapel, was an important area of chapel activity. When Reverend Jabez Bunting, then chairman of the Leeds and Wakefield district, visited Wakefield to give a sermon in aid of its work, on 27 May 1813, it was reported as teaching 500 poor children at a cost of £300 a year. Before there was any extensive provision for weekday elementary education, Sunday schools provided a basic education and well as a religious one. 1827 saw the issue of a new routine for the circuit's Sunday schools: pupils were to arrive at 9.00am for registration, singing and prayers; they attended the morning service at 10.00am and this was followed by lessons; at 1.00pm the school reopened with singing; there was then a scripture lesson followed at 2.00pm by a reading lesson; spelling filled the time from 2.35pm to 3.00pm when there was more reading before the minister or the school governor gave a lecture at 3.40pm; the school closed at 4.00pm. Scholars who wished to undertake Bible studies were taught to write as well as to read. A new Sunday School building was opened on 1 April 1872 (Figure 5).

A missionary society was formed in 1814 with the aim of taking Christianity to Africa and India. Its anniversaries were marked by special sermons, that on 8 May 1825 being given by Reverend Robert Newstead from Ceylon.

Through the 1810s and 1820s, Methodism grew rapidly in Wakefield. In 1813 a preaching station was established for the population of the Westgate area in a warehouse on the corner of Lawefield Lane and Westgate. West Parade members were prominent among the supporters of a chapel at Kirkhamgate; a congregation was meeting there by 1787 when it appears on the newly-formed Circuit list, and by 1818 a building, perhaps on the

Figure 5. A drawing of the Sunday School made in 1975 by I D Wilson. *From the collection of Paul Dawson.*

site of the present village hall, was in use as a chapel. The Wesleyan Chapel of 1818 at Lofthouse was built on land owned by Samuel Stocks, again a West Parade member, and he laid the foundation stone of a new building in 1840, contributing £500 towards its cost. About 1820 the West Parade chapel council decided to begin fund-raising to build a new chapel at Eastmoor. In 1821 a cottage and land were acquired at a cost of £80. The chapel was opened on 20 June 1822, the cost of building being born by subscription. The opening was performed by Reverend Samuel Woolmer and Reverend Thomas Harris, the former being the minister at West Parade. The chapel council then set about raising more funds for the erection of a chapel at Westgate End. This opened on Good Friday, 4 April, 1828 (Figure 6). One of the main subscribers was Robert Drake,

Figure 6. Westgate End Chapel, now the True Vine Fellowship. *From the collection of Paul Dawson.*

a corn merchant who had premises in Kirkgate and who had a shelling plant at Bridge End in partnership as Horner and Drake Co. The chapel had seating for 600, 200 places being free for children of the Sunday school or the poor. There was a large schoolroom under the chapel, capable, it was said, of holding 400.

The centenary of Methodism in Wakefield was celebrated over a four-day period in November 1839. On Monday 28 November there was a public tea in the Corn Exchange attended by 1100 people (Figure 7). The following day children from the Eastmoor, Newton Bar, Westgate End and West Parade Sunday Schools were addressed in the school rooms at West Parade and then led in procession to the Corn Exchange for afternoon tea.

Until the 1820s music at West Parade Chapel was provided by a choir and a small orchestra. In 1805 the Methodist Conference stipulated that 'no instrument of music be introduced into the singers' seats except for a bass viol, should the principal singer require it'. In 1808 the general conference refused to 'sanction or

Figure 7. The Corn Exchange.

consent to the erection of any organs in our chapels'. Where in existence they were not to 'overpower or supersede the singing'. But chapels might have an orchestra to 'guide the singers and congregation'. A consort of flute, clarinet, viol and double bass was advocated. However in 1820 the Methodist Conference agreed to allow larger chapels to install pipe organs. Thus in November 1821 the trustees proposed to erect an organ, with the cost raised by subscription, and to appoint an organist at ten guineas a year. An organ blower was to be paid £1 a year. The organ was built by Joseph Booth (1769-1832) of Gildersome in 1823 and was 'opened' on Sunday 18 January 1824 by Edward Booth, organist at Trinity Church, Leeds. The organ was described as having 'a grand appearance' and 'a fine deep melodic tone'. It had eight stops on the great organ and five on the swell. However in 1827 the Methodist Church council banned the use of organs or other 'mechanical contrivance' for the playing of hymns and psalms, insisting that they must be sung by the human voice alone. The edict was not revoked until 1838.

In 1827 the trustees bought 4,148 square yards of land in Thornhill Croft at 4s (20p) a square yard and 3,352 square yards of this was allocated for a burial ground. It was laid out with flowers, trees and shrubs by Mr Barrett, landscape gardener and trustees of

Figure 8. West Parade burial ground. *Kate Taylor.*

the chapel who gave his services free. The first internment was that of Edwin Cook (aged 36) on 28 August 1829. In 1852 the Board of Health inspector, William Ranger, proposed the closure of all Wakefield's town centre burial ground in the belief that they contaminated the water supply. The grounds surrounding the parish church were particularly condemned. The West Parade ground remained open, however, throughout the chapel's life. It was sold to Wakefield Corporation in 1966 as a peace garden (Figure 8). Finances were always 'tight' and it must have been something of a relief to the chapel stewards when on 24 July 1833 Parliament passed the act which exempted churches and chapels from both the poor rate and the church rate.

The remainder of the land was laid out, by 1851, as Graham Terrace.

During the early 1830s it was decided to enlarge the chapel to cater for the still growing congregation. The Wakefield Methodist Circuit had, it was reported, gained 300 new members in the space of two years. Chapel trustees at West Parade could not supply the demand for 'sittings' (the tenancy of a seat). Work, costing £937, began in 1835 and was completed by 1838. £912 was raised by donations and subscriptions: £100 was donated by Samuel Stocks and £50 each by Joseph Holdsworth and Joshua Swallow. The essentially square building was lengthened making it 96 feet long and 66 feet wide and capable of holding 1,700 people. The architect was

James Simpson of Leeds. At this time the chapel had seven sash windows on each floor on both sides of the building. It had cloth-lined pews and benches with a small white pulpit which had a spiral stair leading to the speaking platform. A new mahogany pulpit was provided, so high that the minister could see into the gallery, and the chapel was lit by gas. Only three of the contractors made any subscription on this occasion and the sums were small:

Tradesmen	Trade	Cost	Subscription
William Kitsman	*mason*	*£50*	*£1*
Samuel Drew	*provided pulpit*	*£20*	*£5 5s*
Joseph Child	*builder*	*£250*	*£5 5s*
Depledge and Speight	*joiners*	*£400*	
Thomas Backhouse	*plumber*	*£55*	
W H Barker	*plasterer*	*£70*	
John Fryston	*roof slater*	*£62*	

The chapel was reopened for worship on 19 October 1838 (Figures 9 and 10).

Shortly afterwards a new organ was installed, the original one being considered too small for the enlarged capacity of the building. This was built by Francis Booth (1802-1874) and was opened on 6 March 1839. Edward Booth, then organist at Brunswick Chapel, Leeds, gave two recitals, one after the morning service the following Sunday and one on the Monday evening, with pieces by Handel, Haydn, Mozart and Purcell.

The organ was enlarged in 1880, by Abbott and Smith of Leeds, from two manuals to three, with the pedal organ enlarged as well, giving a full range of twenty-nine stops. It was opened by Joseph Naylor Osborne Hardy who was by then the organist at Wakefield Parish Church. The alterations cost £440 a part of which was financed from donations. It was enlarged again in 1897 at a cost of £247 when the case was remodelled at a cost of a further £120. The case was described in the *Wakefield Express* at the time as having changed 'from a decidedly unhandsome box to a thing of beauty'.

A Choir Committee was formed in 1872 which had, amongst its responsibilities, the task of appointing the organists. On its first being established it expressed criticism of the limited number of tunes being sung and suggested that 'some of the good, old tunes might be introduced with great advantage to the congregation'. In December 1880 when a number of members of the congregation were invited to form a voluntary choir, it was felt desirable to 'form a class for the instruction in the theory of music, to which members of the choir be admitted free, and members of the congregation on the payment of a fee'. In 1882, to keep standards high, it was decided that prospective choir members should be tested by the choir master and choir secretaries. From 1885 the trustees gave the choir an annual picnic. The committee had power to alter the choir stalls and had them re-arranged in 1896. In 1880 when Isaac Briggs was the choirmaster, the choir had 90 members. In 1898 it was agreed that ministers and other preachers should have a prayer with the choir before the beginning of the service. The average strength of the choir in 1909 was reduced to twenty-six and after the Second World War it was necessary to recruit outside help before any major choral work could be performed.

In fact the chapel was noted for its fine choirs and for its organists and choirmasters including J N O Hardy (1880-1886 when he moved to the parish church), A E S Sugden (1887-1919), J Fox Taylor (1920-1924), Arthur Beevers (1925-1928), N Kenneth Shrigley (1928-?1956), George H Jones (?1956-1960, when he moved to Wesley Hall) and finally Victor Foster (1960-1963). Sugden was a professional music teacher who lived in Arundel Street. When the chapel closed the organ was scrapped.

Figure 9. Map of 1854.

Figure 10. West Parade pulpit, 1900, as altered from the pulpit of 1838. *The John Goodchild Collection.*

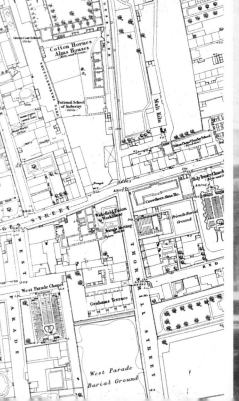

Such was the importance of the organist, or organist/choirmaster, that, at least in the earlier part of the twentieth century, appointments were dealt with by a special sub-committee. When Sugden left in 1919 advertisements, offering a salary of a minimum of £50 a year, were placed in the *Yorkshire Post, Methodist Recorder* and, on 20 January 1920, the *Wakefield Express*. When these proved unsuccessful further advertisements were placed in the *Musical Times* and the *Yorkshire Advertiser*. Arrangements were made for the applicants to be tested by N Coates, organist of Bradford Parish Church, on 20 March. J Fox Taylor, the successful candidate, who had been choirmaster under Sugden, was appointed at £65 a year.

The sub-committee also set the organist's wages, had to pay for the water used to power the instrument until an electric blower was fitted in 1933, and might also arrange organ recitals or the performance of choral works. The terms and conditions set out for the post of organist, or organist/choirmaster, in 1920 included the requirement that the successful candidate should be an ex officio member of the choir committee and must attend all meetings. All choir music had to meet with the approval of the committee.

The organist was allowed to use the organ for tuition but must pay 4d an hour for the water and must not allow the times of lessons to conflict with the times of services.

Elementary schooling was provided, until the *1870 Education Act*, on a voluntary basis by both the Established Church and Non-conformity. At the Methodist National Conference in 1843 the Wesleyans committed themselves to building 700 day schools in the next seven years. A meeting was held at West Parade Chapel on 21 December 1843. This supported the conference decision and a committee was set up to raise funds to build a school. A target of £1,000 was set on the understanding that the chapel trustees would provide a further £300. By 1845 the trustees were able to buy a plot of land measuring 22 yards by 100 yards adjoining Thornhill Street for £590. Plans were prepared by the Barnsley architect, John Whitworth, a prominent Wesleyan who have his services free. The foundation stone was laid on 2 November 1845 by Samuel Stocks. The building cost £1,200. £2,500 was raised by subscription and the school was opened, free of debt, in July 1846 by Reverend B G Macdonald, then minister of West Parade (Figure 11). In the early days pupils came from as far away as Alverthorpe and Newmillerdam and even, in the case of one family, from Normanton. The school moved to a new building in Field Lane, Thornes, in 1974.

Samuel Stocks was one of the leading members of the

congregation. A keen Liberal politically, and ardent supporter of the Wesleyan church, he lived in South Parade. He had made his fortune from a drapery business in Manchester and in 1829 had an annual income of £5,000. He died on 15 October 1850 aged eighty-four and was buried in the family tomb in the north aisle of Rothwell Church. On 18 November a sermon was given in his memory by Thomas Jackson. This was subsequently published by John Mason, 14 City Road, London.

Another early benefactor of the chapel, William Spicer, was constable of Wakefield in 1815. Member of the congregation, George William Harrison, was the first mayor of Wakefield after it became a municipal borough in 1848. Edward Green of the Fuel Economiser works and Phoenix Brass Foundry, who became a baronet in 1886, was a trustee of West Parade in the 1850s. David Colvard, who had set up in practice in the 1780s and was known as the 'honest lawyer', was a steward at the chapel between 1815 and 1822. The celebrated blind lawyer, William Pickard (1829-1865) was another member and was interred in the chapel burial ground. Joseph Holdsworth was a steward of the Wakefield Circuit from 1805-1815 and others of the dyeing family were members. Robert Bownas Mackie, Wakefield's member of Parliament in 1880, and others of his family too were members. Samuel Pickles, a gentleman's outfitter, was appointed a trustee in 1915; he was Mayor of Wakefield in 1930. John Cryer, the bookseller and celebrated antiquarian was a member and was interred in 1864 in the burial ground. Much of the chapel's early history is recorded in his collection of newspaper cuttings and bill posters. John Archer, who set up a matting and flocking business with his brother Jesse, and who built Flanshaw Lodge in the 1920s, was a trustee at West Parade. There were many other influential individuals and there were notable families who, often for more than one generation, worshipped at West Parade, including Browns, Glovers, Pawsons and Leedals.

Perhaps the loftiest connections with the chapel came through

Figure 11. The Methodist School in Thornhill Street. *Kate Taylor*

Reverend George B Macdonald, minister from 1844 to 1847. His four daughters married Sir Edward Burne-Jones, Sir Edward Poynter, Reverend Joseph Kipling (father of the poet Rudyard Kipling) and Alfred Baldwin (father of Stanley, Viscount Baldwin, the prime minister in 1923-4, 1924-29 and 1935-37).

Throughout the late Victorian period Methodist zeal flourished. In the 1880s other denominations besides the Methodists were rebuilding or 'renewing' their chapels. Funds to renovate the interior of West Parade were raised throughout the 1870s, in particular via bazaars, which raised £1,114. 10s 3d. In 1880 the old cloth-lined pews and benches were removed and replaced with matching oak ones, with the gallery front being re-styled in polished oak as well. The pulpit was remodelled. Figures 12 and 13). The vestibule and minister's and choir vestries were added. A further renovation was proposed in 1896. While the work was carried out, between 6 April and 23 May 1897, services were held in the Corn Exchange. One of the key innovations was the installation of electric lighting; this cost £143 14s with a further £66 5s 8d being paid for a generator. The work also included new carpets, and new paving and flagging at the front and side of the building.

In the latter part of the nineteenth century and the earlier part of the twentieth century chapels provided a substantial social life as well as spiritual nurture. West Parade had a guild which met monthly and provided a wide range of cultural and fund raising activities including sports. A badminton club was formed in 1925 and a tennis club in 1933. There was also a ladies' 'sewing bee' which raised money for the chapel by its needlework.

Membership of the chapel began to fall in the early years of the twentieth century. In 1929 the pulpit was converted from the double-decker of 1880 to a rostrum, as there were no longer enough

Figure 12. The Interior of West Parade c 1870s.

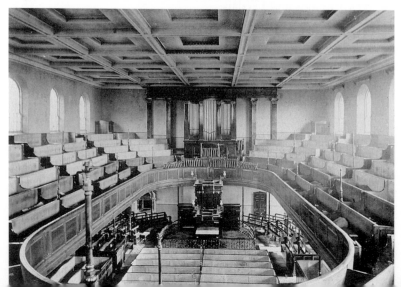

attending services to fill the gallery (Figure 14).

The building of the large Lupset housing scheme in the 1920s and early 1930s provided the incentive to build a place of worship close to it. Dewsbury Road Primitive Methodist Chapel was opened in 1929. However the Wesleyans erected an old wooden army hut, bought for £600 from the South Yorkshire Methodist mission at Goldthorpe, at the end of Thornes Road, opening it on 1 February 1928. This was replaced after the act of union which combined the Wesleyan, Primitive and Free Methodist Churches, by Wesley Hall. The foundation stone of the Hall was laid on 1 December 1934. The building was designed to be chapel, theatre or cinema (it had a box), Sunday school and youth club.

In 1946 the trustees built a new house in Agbrigg for the minister, at a cost of £1,500. The debt had not been cleared at the time of the chapel's closure.

Figure 13. Interior as shown in the Methodist Recorder of 1900.
From the collection of Paul Dawson.

After the Second World War, West Parade and Grove Road chapels were threatened with closure and it was proposed that the Grove Road members, of which there were 78 in 1956, should join West Parade which had some 148 members.

In 1961 the trustees proposed demolishing the chapel and building a new one on the same site but the scheme came to nothing. West Parade closed its doors to worship in 1963 after the building

Figure 14. Interior 1941

Figure 15. Trinity Methodist Church, 1999. *Kate Taylor*

was declared unsafe: there was dry rot in the roof, the wiring was faulty, and the ceiling plaster was liable to fall. It was estimated that over £4,000 would be needed to make it safe. Between 1963 and 1966 the congregation met in the schoolroom. Proposals were made to unite Brunswick Chapel, Grove Road and West Parade but again this came to nothing and on 9 October 1966 the final service was held. The remaining congregation went either to Brunswick Chapel or to Grove Road. However Grove Road chapel, the last inner-city Methodist chapel in Wakefield, itself closed on 8 September 1978. The Eastmoor, Brunswick and Grove Road congregations were united in the new Trinity Methodist Church which opened in 1984 (Figure 15).

Once West Parade was closed, its assets were sold. These included Graham Terrace, off Thornhill Street, the manse, the Sunday School and the burial ground. The manse and graveyard are all that have survived into 1999.

The day school, however, remains virtually unchanged.

In 1993 three of the chapels remaining in the West Parade Circuit merged to form the West Wakefield Methodist Circuit, housed in the Primitive Methodist Chapel in Dewsbury Road.

Sources

Baines' *Yorkshire Directory*, 1822.
W S Banks, *Walks about Wakefield*, 1871
J Batty, *A History of Rothwell*, 1877
The Brown family archive.
Brunswick Chapel centenary brochure, 1976.
The *Cambridge Encyclopaedia*.
Henry Clarkson, *Memories of Merry Wakefield*, 1887.
The Cresswell family archive.
The Cryer Collection, Wakefield Library Headquarters.
The *Dictionary of National Biography*.
The *Methodist Recorder*, 1906.
J Newsome, ms *History of Methodism in Wakefield*, 1963.
Kate Taylor (ed), *Wakefield District Heritage*, 1976.
Trade Directories
The *Wakefield Express*.
The *Wakefield Free Press*.
The *Wakefield and Halifax Journal*.
The *Wakefield Journal* and *West Riding Herald*.
The *Wakefield Star*.
Memorials in West Parade burial ground.
J W Walker, *A History of Wakefield Cathedral*, 1905
J W Walker, *Wakefield, its History and its People*, 1939.
West Parade Trustees' Minute Book, 1900-1931, West Yorkshire Archive Service, Wakefield.

10. Shops and Street Traders in Outwood in the 1930s

by Norman Ellis

TWICE A YEAR MANY HOUSEWIVES brought out a small box in which had been placed little coloured pieces of paper known as Co-op checks. Each bearing the customer's membership number, they were receipts for the amount of money spent during the previous six months at branches of the Wakefield Borough Co-operative Society. When the dividend was declared - about three shillings (15p) in the pound in the 1930s - it was possible to determine how much bonus had accrued. Some families earmarked the bounty to pay for a holiday or buy Christmas presents; others chose to invest the 'divi' in their Co-op account and accumulate interest.

The central premises of the Wakefield Borough Co-perative Society, which was first registered in 1867, were in Horbury Road, Wakefield. Branches were opened at Alverthorpe and Sandal and later at Outwood and Lupset. The Outwood branch was on Leeds Road, near the top of Bolus Lane. In the 1930s Sidney Smith, a burly man, was manager of the large, well-stocked shop. His assistants included Tommy Clapham and Harry Burton. Bacon was cut on a dangerous-looking slicer, butter was patted into shapes, sugar was scooped into blue bags, and biscuits were weighed out. Bulky groceries could be ordered for delivery later in a brown paper parcel by one of the blue CWS vehicles. A shop annexe contained the

Figure 1. Outwood Chuch Institute and the local branch shop of the Wakefield Industrial Co-operative Society on the right, c1930. *Norman Ellis*

outfittings and haberdashery department, looked after by Miss Gascoigne and later by Miss Marshall.

In competition locally with the CWS was the WIS or Wakefield Industrial Society, with central premises in Westgate in Wakefield. It had numerous branches in the Wakefield area, their modest Outwood shop being in Argyle Terrace on Leeds Road, near the Church Institute (Figure 1). An agent toured the Outwood area to collect orders for subsequent delivery. Their vehicles were painted bright red. Like the Borough Co-op the WIS paid 'divi'.

Those people who did not buy their groceries at the Co-ops may have used Lindley's Stores. The shop, on Leeds Road in an area known locally as the Hollow, was just around the corner from Annie Street. Arthur Lindley, who had married my mother's sister, Amy, took over the premises in the mid 1920s. Living quarters were at the back of the shop and upstairs. The store facade had two windows and a central door, the grocery area being to the right. Talk about getting a quart into a pint! So much merchandise was crammed into the modest space that it seemed even smaller than it was. Goods were frequently manoeuvred via a trap door from the cellar storeroom. The grocery section did a brisk trade, but Arthur Lindley, a man of drive and initiative, developed the shoe, boot and cobbling section behind the other window (Figure 2). A further development was the opening of a branch a few doors further up which sold hardware, electrical goods, bicycles and, as Christmas approached, a wide range of quality toys. Arthur's elder son, George, was placed in charge. The grocery shop was eventually managed by younger son, Harold.

Arthur Lindley's stores were part of a block of shops which also included George Boott, hairdresser, and Leonard Godfrey, fried-fish dealer. Leonard, a jovial, friendly man, had taken over the business from Mr and Mrs Chauvet. Fried fish cost twopence, chips were a penny. I preferred the fish cakes or, better still, the collops, which

Figure 2. Lindley's Stores, c1930. *Norman Ellis Collection.*

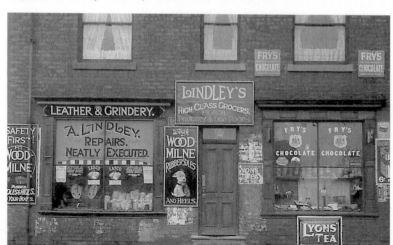

were slices of potato fried in batter and which cost, I believe, twopence for eight.

I had my curly locks (where did they go?) cut by Mr Boott once every four weeks, usually after school, for fourpence. The benches along two sides of the shop were often filled with ten or more waiting clients, in which case I buried my head in the *Rainbow* or other of the comics which were strewn about. Mr Boott used a 'cut-throat' razor for shaving. Most men required this service towards the end of the week, especially on a Saturday. On hot days, whilst working, Mr Boott drank a mixture of lemonade and milk. His wife did some ladies' hairdressing. The other local barber was Fred Smith of Newton Hill, a lame but kind and friendly man.

Outwood's best known cobbler, Arthur Ellis (no relation of mine), worked in a dark, low wooden hut opposite the *Queen Hotel* on Leeds Road. A good cobbler, but a man of few words, he was the most laid-back character I have ever known. Taking the boots or shoes for repair was relatively easy; collecting them was more complicated: 'Are Mrs Smith's shoes ready?' Long pause. Signs of movement. Slow search. 'Are these em?' 'No.' More searching. 'What about these?' 'No, they had a buckle.' Longer pause. Longer search. In fairness, the footwear always turned up. The situation improved slightly when Albert Ogden, who lived in the Avenue, was employed there for a period.

Slightly further up the hill from the Borough Co-op, but at the same side, were the bakery and shop of Thomas Ramsden, where choice bread, teacakes, potted meat, sausage rolls, vanilla slices and other delicacies were produced. Further up still was the chemist shop of Tom Butterfield, who had a monopoly in the area for pills, potions and prescriptions.

The Thrift Stores, situated on Leeds Road at the opposite side of Annie Street to Lindley's Stores, was part of a big grocery chain which had branches throughout the West Riding. George Scott had a grocery shop in the Newton Hill area, on the left-hand side of Leeds Road going towards Wakefield.

Bertram Horner was a grocer and beer retailer at the top of Newton Lane. His sons, Tom and Bernard, were about the same age as me. Earlier in the century this grocery shop belonged to A A Illingworth, when it also housed the Post Office (Figure 3). Postal facilities were later transferred a short distance down Leeds Road to Mrs Alice Clayton's small grocery shop.

A wooden hut near the top of Bolus Lane, approximately eight feet square, housed the premises of Charles Holroyd, better known as

Tinner Holroyd. He repaired pans and peggy tubs at a time when housewives could not afford to buy new ones.

Two blocks of buildings, each of which housed several shops, stood at the Leeds Road end of Ledger Lane. The blocks were divided by Queen Street, which ran down to Annie Street. On the corner with Leeds Road was the newsagency of Charlie Swain, where sweets and chocolate were also sold. Charlie's son Leslie was a bit older than me.

Slightly further up was the bread, cake and confectionery shop of the Sykes family from Lofthouse Gate. They specialised in catering for weddings and dances. Still in the same block and on the corner with Queen Street was Mrs Florence Berridge's grocery shop. Mrs Berridge's daughter, Eileen, was about my age and the two sons slightly younger.

The first shop in the next block belonged to Mrs Edith Gilchrist, who specialised in cheap sweets and other sugary treats which were so beloved by children. The shop, being near the council school in Ledger Lane, seemed to corner the market amongst the youngsters. As well as chewing gum, bubble gum, dolly mixtures and jelly babies, kali (pronounced kay-lie), which was a sherbet powder, was popular. A small paper bag of kali cost a ha'penny. A sherbet fountain, which was a packet of kali with a tube of liquorice through which it was

sucked, cost a penny. Another shop in this block sold fish and chips.

Much further up Ledger Lane, opposite the Grange, and inconspicuous amongst rows of houses, was the village's other Post Office and general shop which was managed by Miss Jane Ethel Wilson and her assistant, Maud Barstow. My mother occasionally sent me here, not just for stamps but for two ounces of yeast to bake the bread.

For buying everyday commodities Outwood was self-sufficient. Wakefield and Leeds were accessible by bus or train for larger items such

Figure 3. The Post Office, Leeds Road, c1930. *Norman Ellis Collection.*

as furniture, the buying of which was usually prefaced by shop-window gazing and price comparisons. For many folk a shopping spree in Wakefield, even for the lesser items, was an antidote to the dull routine. Who could resist going to Redman's in Upper Kirkgate for fresh-sliced bacon or loose dried fruit from an excellent counter display? The Saturday market, which lasted into the evening, was second to none.

The streets of Outwood were enlivened by the sight and sound of various travelling traders, such as milkmen, greengrocers, fish vendors and ice-cream purveyors. Milkmen came virtually every day. There was no green-top, red-top or white-top. Milk was brought to the door in a large can and ladled into the housewife's jug or basin. It was stored in the coolest part of the house, either the cellar or the pantry. Jeremiah (Jerry) Green, a big, red-cheeked milkman who looked every inch a farmer, lived at Springfield Farm near the top of Lingwell Gate Lane. He was assisted on the farm and with his milk round by his two sons. James Holroyd Hallas and family had a dairy farm opposite the *Queen Hotel*, Leeds Road. Their grazing land was at Lingwell Gate. In summer the cows were brought back to the farm every day for milking, but in winter they were kept at the farm permanently. Pigs were reared, their 'pong' frequently wafting over the Bolus Lane area. I do not recall that this Hallas family ever delivered milk locally. However Richard (Dick) Hallas and family delivered milk from their farm opposite the *Victoria Hotel*, which was also on Leeds Road. Their several areas for cow grazing included land in Outwood Park. This Hallas family also had a coal business.

For many years my mother bought her milk from George Cox, a dairyman on Canal Lane, Lofthouse Gate, who eventually took his sons into the business. Like other milkmen he traversed the streets with horse and float. Mr Cox, a small, wiry man, coaxed his horse with aniseed balls (and occasionally gave me some).

Figure 4. Robert Lee, the pot man from Robin Hood. *Norman Ellis Collection.*

In 1932 the Wakefield Borough Co-operative Society opened a model dairy, complete with pasteurising plant, on the edge of Lupset. They became the largest milk retailers in Wakefield, and revolutionised deliveries in and around the town, including Outwood. The pint bottles, with a cardboard top and punch-hole, became a common sight on many doorsteps.

Almost as familiar as the milkmen were the greengrocers. Fred Wood had a greengrocery business in Ledger Lane, almost opposite the old girls' school. With his horse-drawn four-wheeled covered cart, Mr Wood covered several areas twice a week. In the late 'thirties' the business was taken over by Charlie Moss. George Webster, described as a fruiterer, also had a round and operated from Bolus Lane. Eventually they were joined by Mr Holroyd from the Lofthouse area, with his open cart.

After the Russell family took over Broomhall Farm, which was near Snow Hill at Wrenthorpe, George Russell regularly carted his fruit and vegetables up to various parts of the Outwood. George, a devout Methodist and local preacher, subsequently died in tragic circumstances.

A man nicknamed 'Tatie Buyers' came around with his potatoes crying, 'Tatie buyers, fifteen pounds a shilling'.

A regular weekly visitor with his horse-propelled covered four-wheel cart was the pot man, actually Robert Lee, a china and glass dealer from Robin Hood (Figure 4). In addition to all manner of pots and pans, a large drum of paraffin was carried, which had a tap for transferring the widely used liquid to the customer's receptacle.

Before the days of 'fridges and freezers, the street ice-cream vendors cornered much of the product's market. Outwood's own ice-cream man was Charlie Beales. The ice cream was made in the yard near the old smithy, which was opposite the lodge gates at the bottom of Outwood Park. In value for money, old Brayshaw, of Italian appearance, was hard to beat. He came from Leeds and, standing in

Figure 5. Leeds Road, Outwood, looking north from Victoria Corner, c1930. *Norman Ellis Collection*

the back of his horse-drawn float, seemed a giant of a man. In contrast, William Quinn, from Main Street, East Ardsley, was of lean appearance and not generous with his ice cream. Unlike other ice-cream vendors who used horse-propelled carts, Eldorado and Walls ('Stop me and buy one') employed men with cycles. The Walls' contraption was a tricycle with a large box at the front. The triangular sectioned fruit-flavour ice bars, surrounded by a cardboard tube, were favourite children's fare at one penny each. They were a forerunner of ice lollies. If you only had a ha'penny you bought half a bar. The Eldorado man had a bicycle with a smaller box at the front. His fare included small fruit-flavour bricks, but they were not as popular as the Walls' ice bars.

Eventually Lumbs, Lunns and Massarellas arrived on the scene with brightly painted covered-over carts, still with horses, but subsequently replaced by gaily painted motor vehicles. Lumbs produced delicious traditional ice cream at their Sandal dairy, not the soft sort which is popular today. Every day except Sunday I ran out with my tumbler for a pennyworth, which included two wafer biscuits.

Some of the ice-cream men came every day. A favourite parking spot was outside the school on Ledger Lane. Headmaster Murray did not like this, partly because of the litter on the road and in the playground, but was powerless to stop it. Those Walls cardboard tubes got everywhere!

The ability of fish sellers to get wet cod or herring to your door before it went off was a minor miracle. The secret was plenty of ice. The village's fish salesmen included Fish Liza and Paddy Hare, a tall man with ginger hair whose stock embraced mussels and other shellfish. In summer he hawked ice cream, and called out 'Okey pokey' which was the old name for it. This gave rise to the rhyme:

> *Okey pokey, penny a lump.*
> *That's the stuff to make you jump*

There was another version of the couplet. A man sold yeast (we pronounced it 'yest') door to door. He was partly disabled and carried the yeast in a wicker basket on his disabled arm. Mr Davies, who was Jack Asquith's grandfather and lived in the Avenue, went round selling flowers from large cardboard boxes, mainly to regular customers, thus raising a bit of 'baccy' money. Mr Garrett, who also dwelt in the Avenue, trundled round with paperback books in a case, a kind of travelling library.

Clifford Swaine, who lived in Princess Street and frequently had a cigarette in his mouth, used to visit the cemetery to gather soft shale known as scouring stone. Housewives rubbed it on the stone steps outside their houses. Clifford could sell a barrowful quickly.

Rag-and-bone men, who also took old iron and virtually anything on which they saw a chance of profit, were habitual visitors, usually hollering as they steered their carts along the street, but occasionally knocking on the door. Many of the rags were sold and auctioned for the manufacture of mungo and shoddy in the nearby Dewsbury area. Some of the more enterprising ragmen, especially those who possessed a motor van or truck, stood outside the school in Ledger Lane at dinner time (in the middle of the day) and handed each pupil a leaflet stating that, in exchange for a bag of rags, they would receive a gift, such as a celluloid whistle, tiny goldfish or day-old chick. I sometimes managed to persuade my mother to part with the rags we were not still wearing and duly exchanged them. I never got a fluffy chicken. Doubtless they were young cockerels which were otherwise unsaleable. I heard stories of people trying to keep the poor creatures alive in front of the fire or in a cool oven. But they always died.

Most of the ragmen owned a horse and cart, but Barrow Lizzie pushed a handcart. Tall, with long, dark clothes, a man's flat cap and a permanent scowl, she looked quite tyrannical. Did she really wear some of the cast-off clothing which she received?

Without doubt Outwood's best-known street characters were Billy Leather and Firewood Arthur, each of whom possessed an ample portion of simple entrepreneurial flair. Billy Leather, lean in appearance, sincere and straightforward in his dealings, operated from the yard behind the old smithy on Victoria Corner, where numerous discarded household items were kept (Figure 5). Anyone wanting an old peggy tub for the garden could usually obtain one for two or three pence. Billy did light carting in the area, usually charging half-a-crown, whatever the load or distance. My father once bought a large second-hand earthenware sink at Kilkenny's, who had a yard up Rishworth Street in Wakefield. The problem was how to get the object back to Outwood. Billy Leather obliged and accordingly received his half-crown. The sink was required for a couple of ducks to bathe in. They never laid a single egg. Their only notable achievement was splashing (and quacking) in the middle of the night, to the annoyance of our neighbours.

Firewood Arthur, or Arthur Firewood, whose real name was Arthur McLennan, collected firewood, made out of old pit props, from the yard at Lofthouse Colliery and carted it round Outwood and district where it was much in demand for lighting the many coal fires. For his favourite customers, including those who supplied him with a mug of hot tea, Arthur chopped the wood into sticks suitable for kindling. His handcart was a tall squarish wooden box on two wheels, one of which was larger than the other and gave the contraption a sideways slant. Arthur was small, wiry and splayfooted and wore a flat cap. He lodged for a time in York Street in Wakefield. Of his various landladies, some treated him better than others, even feeding him with steak and chips. Each day, when work was over, Arthur left his barrow in a convenient location, ready for the start of the next day's work. As children we taunted Arthur, perhaps regarding him as an older playmate. He did not seem to mind unduly, but on occasions started to chase us.

Many stories unfolded around Arthur. Once he was seen by Mr Corden, the colliery manager, leaving the pit yard with an empty cart. Asked the reason, Arthur replied, 'No firewood today for Arthur'. Mr Corden took him back to the woodyard and decreed that under no circumstances must Arthur even be sent away without firewood. On another day Arthur was seen grovelling among the pit props on hands and knees muttering, 'Arthur lost a tanner', which used to be a princely sum. On Leeds Road his cart once became fastened in the tramlines. When the tram driver rang his bell, Arthur retorted, 'You can wait. I was here first'.

Arthur retired to an old people's home in Wakefield but, before he died, aged about 93, was lovingly brought back several times to parties at Outwood Memorial Hall, where he met old customers.

Tingalary men played their instruments in the streets. These were street pianos which worked by turning a handle. They were hired from a man in Leeds called Tomasso. Tramps sang in the open to earn a few coppers. Gypsies came to the door selling clothes pegs and lavender and told your fortune

11. WALTER HAMPSON, DIALECT POET

by Peter Wood

IN THE GRAVEYARD of Normanton Parish Church stands a tall rusticated stone memorial (Figure 1). It bears the inscription:

> *Walter Hampson*
> *Dialect poet and writer.*
> *Born April 24th. 1864 Died February 3rd. 1932*
> *He made the best use of life,*
> *and was not afraid of death.*[1]

There will be few people of Normanton or even in Yorkshire who have not heard of this remarkable self-educated man who gave so much pleasure in words to a generation fast declining, and showed that from humble beginnings, if one had the determination, it was possible to make one's mark in society. Hampson did just that, for he was acclaimed by many as 'Yorkshire's Mark Twain'.[2]

Walter Hampson had none of the benefits of an upper or middle class upbringing, with the accepted standard of education that would have gone with either social scale. His education was from an 'elderly woman' at what would be a dame school, from the age of four or five until he was nearly eight when he had a few months more education under a master. He then started work. His father would have been keen, as many parents in that Victorian period were, to get another wage earner in the family, for there were already three brothers and one sister older than him with yet another four siblings to follow.

Walter's character and ideals were laid down by his mother, father, grand-father, great-grand father and even by his great, great, grand-father. Such was the teaching of these relatives and their mode of life that

Figure 1. The memorial to Walter Hampson in Normanton Churchyard. *Peter Wood*

Walter could find no better aim in life but to try to match them.

When Walter wrote the *Clock Almanack for 1922* he put into verse for the month of September a poem for his mother:

> *Gentle Jane! We love her well,*
> *The reason why I scarce can tell;*
> *Her placid, patient, gentle face*
> *Seems radiant with angelic grace.*
> *Her smile, so tender, sweet and calm,*
> *Sheds all around a soothing balm;*
> *Her eyes beam with the light of love*
> *Which comes I know, for heaven above.* [3]

From his mother he learnt patience, love and understanding, for his daughter can not remember a single instance of her father raising either his hand or voice to any of his children, although to emphasise a point he was making he would thump the table top. It should be borne in mind that Mr Hampson as a railway worker would have worked shifts and for weeks on end and may have, at these times, had little contact with the family. His travels, and Union activities, again lessened the family contact, but it would be his dedication to his writings, which he would have been composing or researching, that would have isolated him still further from any family arguments and the problems of children growing up.

At moments when he was not so occupied, he would lead his children around the room while he played on a tin whistle. He had the ability to pick up and play a tune, on the small organ, or the piano, both of which were kept in the front room. The children enjoyed the moments when he would recite a new poem or comic story, using both physical and facial expressions to emphasise either the comedy or drama of the narrative.

People had to make their own home entertainment prior to the radio, and in the Hampson household that was no problem. Most of his children could play some kind of musical instrument. Herbert the eldest son, besides being a teacher of violin and a conductor, wrote for the *Sheffield Free Press*, the *Barnsley Independent* and the *Barnsley Free Press*, and published *Records of a Barnsley Boy Naturalist*. Alice, his eldest daughter, was trained in elocution, and had the skill to converse and write in the Yorkshire dialect, often working and performing alongside Walter. These were only two of the musical Hampson family. With such talent in the family, it was not surprising that Walter was able organise concert parties to entertain and raise money for the Wakefield blind, for many years, with family and friends participating.

Walter's father, Livesey, born around 1830, was a bootmaker, who was still at his last in 1908, when he was working from Westfield Market in Normanton. Livesey was a skilled workman who took great pride in his trade as boot-maker, but he had that independent spirit of a self-employed tradesman which was to keep him poor all his life. He had married Jane Newton Folds, the daughter of a shoe-maker living in Yorkshire, but whose family had originated from Derbyshire. In later life, Jane's father would manage to save enough cash to take over an inn with a small-holding to supplement his income and no doubt help his daughter.

The grand-father Charles, born 1800 or thereabouts, was the first of the family to be a shoe maker. He died in about 1886, so he would have been able to have a personal influence on the young Walter. Charles was a Chartist, and would have been well aware of the Peterloo massacre of 1819. He had regarded the Church of England and the squirearchy as being the leading contenders for all that was wrong in England. He was not, however, blind to the intemperance of some of the working class who could and did spend an inordinate percentage of their wages upon drink. At the age of 26 he became a total abstainer and worked hard as a temperance reformer.

John Hampson, the great grand-father, became a Nonconformist lay preacher, although he had lost the sight of both eyes after losing the sight of one at the age of six by a thrown stone. He was taught basket making and mat weaving sufficiently well to support a wife and family, but he needed the assistance of his grand-daughter to lead him to the villages around Rothwell when he was preaching. His father, also called John, was a friend and associate of John Wesley, whom he accompanied on his preaching missions starting in 1739. It was this Hampson that, if the story is correct, witnessed Wesley having his hair pulled out by Mrs Wesley, who was accustomed to bouts of fits.

These were the ways of life that Walter Hampson gathered from his ancestors and, throughout his life, their teachings seem to have been remembered. He never drank alcohol, and on his death-bed, when one of his daughters thought to moisten his lips with brandy, Walter was heard resolutely to say, 'Have never drunk in all my life and am not starting now'.

Walter was born at Rothwell on 24 April 1864. After his eighth birthday he was sent to work at a local rope works, for a wage of two shillings for a six-day week. The hours could be extended, without extra pay, if a job had to be finished. When he was nine, the family moved to Normanton. No rope works, so Walter had another nine months of schooling. There was to be no more school after this and Walter realised that if he was to improve himself, he would have to be his own teacher. He had learnt to read and write by the age of ten sufficiently well to do just that, and his later life is a tribute to his skill in teaching himself and also to his determination to succeed.

It is not known what jobs young Walter worked at in the local district, but eventually he migrated to Sharlston where he married Eliza Chapell, in 1884. She was two years his junior, from Mapplewell, and they went to live at 10 Crossley Street. While at Sharlston he worked on the coke ovens, itself a dirty and smelly job, but he refused to work underground. His next job was to work for the Lancashire and Yorkshire Railway Company at Normanton as a cleaner. This meant that a change of residence was needed, and for a short time he and his wife rented some rooms with a Mrs Jones, shop keeper on Wakefield Road. With a little more money coming in from his promotion to fireman, he was able to rent a house, in a row known as Railway Houses in Portland Street, which was one of the streets behind Wakefield Road. It was there that five of their children were born.[4]

In the railway system, promotions were through 'links', starting at the bottom link in which he, as a trainee fireman would help to work the station engine. Gradually progressing to higher links would mean firing locomotives going some distance from the home station, and even lodging over-night or possibly for longer. Examinations had to be passed at various stages, and when one was on the top link, it was then possible to take examinations to become a driver. The successful new driver then found himself at the bottom link again, but on a higher rate of pay than when he had been there as a fireman. A locomotive driver was regarded as being at the top, his skill was respected and he would have a financially better life style, than many of his neighbours.

Walter at 35 had become an engine-driver, and was to remain one until he retired at 65 when he was presented with a gold pocket watch by the company. Unfortunately this watch, the clock given for his union activities, and other memorabilia have been scattered amongst his children and can now be considered lost to the local history. With this promotion, and an increase in his pay, another change of address was needed, for there was always some class division in the railway. Cleaners lived in the lower rented accommodation, but by the time a man was a driver he should be buying his own house. The chosen establishment for the Hampson household was 151 Church Lane, later to be re-numbered 133 (Figure 2). The houses on Church Lane reflected the growing prosperity of the residents. There were other older established drivers and railway personnel mixed with a scattering of professionals and trades people. It was here where the Hampsons' other two children were born.[5]

To get the deposit for this house, Eliza had joined the Co-op which had a branch in West Street. The Hampsons never drew the dividend that would be paid yearly on goods that they had purchased. When they had £25 saved up at the Co-op, this was used for the deposit on the Church Lane house. Such was the thrift of Eliza, 'She could make a meal out of a dish-cloth', that she was able to buy a house for one daughter in Leeds.[6] Walter himself bought two houses next to each other for £250 each for the two eldest girls, Alice and Gertrude May.

Walter had joined the National Union of Railwaymen and readily accepted a request to become the Normanton branch secretary, for in it he could see the opportunity to help his fellow man. From this position In later life he worked hard to get compensation for injured colleagues, and strove to get improvements of pay and conditions. He stayed in the Union for over thirty years in one capacity or another. In his representative role he would travel to London, Manchester and Wakefield, to argue with either railway management or Union officials. After one difficult and prolonged confrontation with the management, Walter secured a three shillings a day increase for a group of Normanton railway men who reciprocated by presenting Walter with a clock on which was a suitable inscription of their gratitude.

Walter Hampson stayed at the Normanton sheds all his railway working life, except for one short period when he was transferred to the sheds at Belle Vue.

Walter's extensive travels on union business and experiences in conferences, meetings and work, brought him into contact with Jimmy Thomas of the Union and George Hughes, engineer of Lancashire and Yorkshire Railway and others with whom he could ready converse and reason.[7] He started to get the *Daily Herald* in 1919, and remained

Figure 2. 133 Church Lane, Normanton, the home of Walter Hampson from 1908-1932. *Peter Wood*

loyal to the Labour paper for the rest of his life. Although staunch Labour and a Union official, he refused on several occasions to sit for a safe seat on Normanton Council. Possibly, after he had helped to set up Normanton's Old Men's Parliament, he felt that they had as much chance of creating change as the town council had. He did take a part in local affairs, for as a Union official he was elected to serve on Normanton and District Trades Council and the Old Age Committee. Walter also served on Normanton's Free Library Committee, not only giving them the benefit of his experience and the proof in the value of reading, but to support the movement and ideas he would go around the town with his collection box.

In the early part of the twentieth century, holidays in England may have been considered a rarity and an adventure for the average man, but Walter was not the average person, for he was at heart a traveller. One of the subsidiary departments of the Coop was the Co-operative Holiday Association which organised holidays abroad and tours. Through them, before the out-break of the First World War Walter and Eliza had been to France, Jersey, Ireland and Wales. When some form of normality had returned to the continent of Europe, Walter again went on his travels, but now it was men-only excursions. He went with his two close friends, Dick and Billy, two of Walter's sons, Herbert and Percy, plus his son-in-law, Mr Dunford, the son of the sweet manufacturer of Normanton. They went to France, Holland, Belgium, Switzerland and Italy. In Italy it was Rome and the Vatican that Walter visited and at the latter he claimed that he had had a short talk with the Pope. The excursion to Switzerland cost 37 guineas (£37 85p) for the ten days. In 1932 he, Herbert and friends sailed on the Cunard *RMS Carintha* to Spain. The crossing of the Bay of Biscay was rough, but Walter had no trouble with the movement of the ship; he was the only one not to be sea-sick! Walter's wife was quite content to stay at home looking after the rest of the children at this time.

When he had retired from the railway, Walter took Eliza to Holland for a holiday, even though he would only be drawing the 26 shillings (£1 30p) pension or 'Lloyd George' (Figure 3). It was not extravagant for Walter to spend what

Figure 3. Walter Hampson in his early 60s.

seems large amounts of money on his holidays. He would call his holidays 'doing research'. The seven children that Hampson had had would have made the cost of a family holiday prohibitive, but by this time there was only the youngest daughter at home. When he had reached higher links, Walter was able to give his wife £4 a week, pay the rates and for the coal, keeping the remainder for his own and family treats. His travelling expenses were paid from the cash he received from his writing, and from what he saved by not drinking.

When he was about to set out on an overseas journey, he would get out his 'cruising clothes', his best suit in a navy blue cloth, hand made by a Mr Levy from Leeds. Levy would have measured Walter in his home. Eliza and the children were also measured and clothed by Levy. Walter's shirts, with which he would wear any one of the three types of collars that were in vogue, and other garments, especially the white handkerchiefs for his top pocket, he purchased from his friend Dick. Some of his experiences of overseas travel he used in the his book *Tykes Abroad* published in 1911, in which he uses the Yorkshire dialect by which he would make his name.

The characters in this book are 'Dick Widdup' and 'Billy Swaddles' who accompany Joss, (the name Walter gives himself), on his journey. 'Billy' was William Roberts, a near neighbour living at 129 Church Lane, and 'Dick' was John Richard Eccles, a shop keeper from Lee Brigg (Figure 4). These three men became life-long friends, Billy and Dick often accompanied Walter on his walks around the locality, and they had bicycling holidays together.

Their exploits in *Awheel in Wharfeland* are an example of a cheap touring holiday possibly taken during the First World War, when Walter was at least in his mid-fifties (Figure 5). The three men carried all that they thought they would need to make the journey comfortable including methylated spirit, lamp, kettle, tea-pot and enamelled drinking mugs. In a leather bag were carried tins of fruits,

Figure 4. Walter Hampson with his friend Dick Eccles in the stocks at Kirkthorpe.

milk and fish, drinking cocoa, coffee, tea and treacle. The third member carried cameras and some fifty photographic plates, together with guide books of the areas that they were going to explore. Walter and his two companions cycled in suits, collar and tie, boots and trilby (Figure 6). Each man carried a good 'mac' and one spare shirt, in case it rained!

Awheel in Wharfeland simply tells of the week's holiday, describing the local history, the over-night stops, and the people they met. At Cawood Castle they were offered whiskey and cigars by J Wormald JP. At Bilborough Hall they went in search of Guy Fairfax, and were offered tea. In a discussion that Walter had with Mr Fairfax it must have been annoying to hear Fairfax's opinion that the ruination of the country was caused by the rise of the working man and Lloyd George.

Walter was not blind to the changes that were occurring in England but he uses Billy to express his feelings:

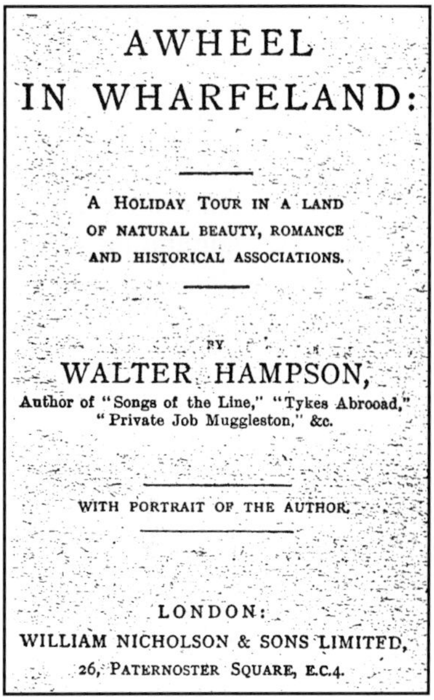

> **AWHEEL IN WHARFELAND:**
>
> A HOLIDAY TOUR IN A LAND
> OF NATURAL BEAUTY, ROMANCE
> AND HISTORICAL ASSOCIATIONS.
>
> ———
>
> BY
> **WALTER HAMPSON,**
> Author of "Songs of the Line," "Tykes Abrooad,"
> "Private Job Muggleston," &c.
>
> ———
>
> WITH PORTRAIT OF THE AUTHOR.
>
> ———
>
> LONDON:
> WILLIAM NICHOLSON & SONS LIMITED,
> 26, PATERNOSTER SQUARE, E.C.4.

Figure 5. The title page of A Wheel in Wharfedale. The one-time local printer is here using a London address.

Aye England, owd England, Ah love tha,
Wi' a love 'at each day grows mooare strong.
In mi 'eart tho sinks deeper an' deeper
As years after years rolls along.
An' spite o' thi faults an' thi follies,
Whativver thi fortune may be
In storm or i' sunshine, i' weal or i' woe,
Tha'll allus be lovely to me.

Whether Walter informed Mr Fairfax of his own political leanings towards Labour is unlikely, as he respected other men's beliefs, and would only try to influence them to change by setting an example. His family could always tell if he had been bettered in an argument or discussion, for on his arrival home he would be unusually quiet and hide behind his pipe and smoke his 'Redbreast'.

Walter Hampson would talk to any interested person, and listen to anyone who had conversation of value. His union activities had honed his skills in presenting his side of an argument, while from his love of literature, he would be able to intersperse these arguments with quotations remembered from his admired authors. This love of reading, took him into the books of Dickens, Scott, Kingsley, Lytton, Carlyle and Ruskin, but his great love was for the writings of Robbie Burns and from his study of the man, Walter was in demand to give talks at Burns' Nights. He was unable to resist showing his admiration for this dialect writer, for he brought Burns into *Tykes Abroad* when the three visited 'Madam Two-Swords' and saw a wax-work of the famous Scot.

> *There is noa need for waxwork shows*
> *Thus to immortalise tha,*
> *Whol Bonnie Doon an' Ayr stiil flow*
> *Ten thassand hearts will prize tha*

In 1905, at the age of forty-one, Walter Hampson had his first book published, *Songs of the Line*.[8] This, a privately printed booklet and not written in dialect, was a collection of poems dealing with the life and times of railways and railwaymen, the conditions of the unemployed and other themes. The booklet, dedicated to his fellow railway workers, also contained a poem praising Burns. One of his proudest possessions was a photograph of himself with Ramsay MacDonald taken outside Burns's cottage.

This was followed by the already mentioned *Tykes Abroad* six years later, when, as he was to do in *Awheel in Wharfeland*, he used as characters his two great friends Dick and Billy with himself as Joss (Figures 7 and 8). While they are in London, Joss for Walter, says

Figure 6. Walter Hampson in his usual cycling clothes.

Ah don't think 'at God e'er intended
At some to great wealth should be born,
Wol others should have their lives blended
Wi' poverty, hunger, an' scorn.

Was Walter blaming God now for the things that he had himself been trying to righten or was he blaming the establishment? At home he never went to church but on his travels churches would be part of his itinerary. He had a great respect for the 'old style of Christianity', where people would help those less fortunate. Where a churchman exhibited those qualities, Walter would have the greatest respect but he found that many of them were more interested in their standing in society than in keeping to the teachings of the church.

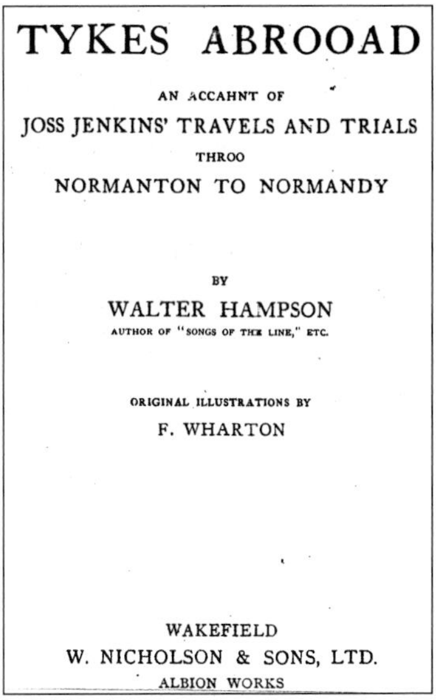

Private Job Muggleston, sub-titled *Fun I' Th' Army* came out in 1916, and was very well received at home and by the troops fighting abroad (Figure 9). He used again a name that he was very familiar with, Dick, although he does give the man a surname of Dunn. Although alive when major conflicts involving England were taking place, Walter was never required to serve in the forces. Whether he was a pacifist at heart or recognised the futility of war is uncertain, but into the mouth of Joe Muggleston he expressed the feeling of many people during the war, and he certainly spoke for the soldiers out in the mud of Flanders;

Ah'm longin', dear Nance, for
that glad day to come
When this cruel war 'll be
ended.
An' peace shall return like a
dove to her nest

TYKES ABROAD

AN ACCAHNT OF
JOSS JENKINS' TRAVELS AND TRIALS
THROO
NORMANTON TO NORMANDY

BY

WALTER HAMPSON
AUTHOR OF "SONGS OF THE LINE," ETC.

ORIGINAL ILLUSTRATIONS BY
F. WHARTON

WAKEFIELD
W. NICHOLSON & SONS, LTD.
ALBION WORKS

Figure 7. The title page of *Tykes Abroad*, printed in Wakefield by the Jacob's Well Lane printer.

Figure 8. F Wharton's 1911 characerisation of Dick, Billy and Joss, for Tykes Abroad.

Wi'all its rich blessings attended.
Mi' heart then will flutter, exalted wi' joy,
Like a bird, fro' its prison set free.
For then Ah s'all leave all this carnage behind
An' return to owd England an' thee.

Walter's only contact with the enemy was taking his children out into a nearby field as a German Zeppelin droned over, yet he had endeavoured to capture the feelings of front line soldiers when Dick Dunn, in a letter to his parents, complains:

When we cam here Ah thowt we'd come on purpose to kill Germans but Ah find Ah wor labourin' under a gurt mistak', for we arn't allahed to touch 'em unless we get orders to do soa.

The book was given a dedication to Bryham Kirkby, but in true Hampson style, Walter found a way of having a laugh when he wrote.;

To
Mi Owd Friend
Bryham Kirkby
This Book Is Inscribed Not Only Becoss Ah Respect
Him Varry Sincerely
But Alsoa Becoss Ah Fancy Ah'm Conferrin'
A Greeat Honor On Missen.[9]

Figure 9. The title page of Private Job Muggleston.

Figure 10. Walter Hampson's own copy of the first Almanack for which he was responsible.

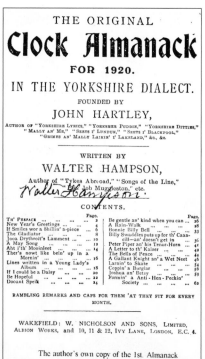

In 1918 Walter was asked to take over the the *Clock Almanack*, a Yorkshire dialect annual magazine although his name only appears on a few of the articles that first year (Figure 10).[10] The *Almanack* was started in 1865 by a Halifax hat shop proprietor named Wilson, and edited by James Bland. Wilson asked John Hartley to be the editor in 1867 and for a few years the magazine was known as the Original Illuminated Clock Almanack due to Mr Wilson having an illuminated clock outside his premises. Over the next few years the title was shortened to the *Original Clock Almanack*. The magazine, when edited by Hampson, all in dialect, contained a calendar with that day's events, a monthly poem, twelve short stories, monthly Rambling Remarks and his Hooamly Filossofy.

It would be around this time that Walter joined the Yorkshire Dialect Society in Leeds, which had been started in Leeds in 1891 by Dr Joseph Wright, but first he had to write a poem, in dialect, prior to his acceptance; this presented no problem to a writer of his calibre.

To concentrate on his writings, in fine weather Walter erected a tent on the back lawn and would settle down to work, only to have the silence broken by his own chuckles. There were many times when, on finishing his shift either late at night or early morning would, once at home, don his favourite red leather slippers and begin to write by the light of a candle. Sometimes he would have the local policeman with him, who had called to see that all was well, and that Walter was not a burglar!

When finished it was the duty of one of his daughters, Millicent, always called Dolly, to take the pieces to Nicholson's in Vicarage Street, Wakefield. His payment for the *Clock Almanack*, normally of 68 pages, was at the rate of seven shillings and sixpence a page.

Walter was also a contributor to the *Railway Review*, edited by G J Wardle, and to the *Normanton Advertiser*. Besides doing short stories for the latter he would devise walks, organise walking parties and then write them up for the paper. His youngest daughter remembers accompanying her father on several of these journeys, often beginning when Walter would arrive home stating that he had booked a bus to go to into the Dales, or the Hebden Bridge area. Regardless of where he led his party, his first action would be to find a suitable farm house where he could order ham and egg teas for the group to be eaten after the walk. Such was his circle of friends, that the coach would be quickly filled, and Walter had another walk to write about. These walk jottings brought him in two guineas a time, which was the same that he received when he went to Manchester, only a few weeks before he died, to read two of his poems on the radio.

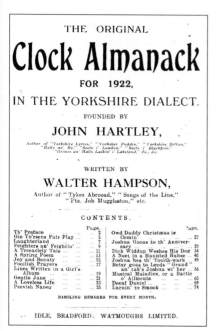

Figure 11. The Almanack of 1922, after the publication had been taken over by Watmoughs.

The last Almanack to which W.H. contributed .

Regardless of the weather, Walter would lead his friends on shorter rambles around his town and surrounding area, gathering information, from friend or stranger; this he was able to use in his *Nomanton Past and Present* serialised in the local paper over 27 weeks. One of his great joys was either walking in the rain or immediately after rain had fallen especially in the Kirkthorpe area. He would don an old trilby, put on leggings and rain coat to take his 'rain walk' in which he was able to enjoy the cleanliness and freshness of the wet day.

The publisher of the *Clock Almanack*, and the one which Walter used for his later books up to the year 1922 was a local firm, W Nicholson and Sons Ltd. at Albion Works, Wakefield. When the magazine was taken over by Watmoughs Ltd at Idle, Bradford, they retained Walter as editor and sole writer for the Clock (Figure 11). Sir Ben Turner M P for Batley and Morley was brought in to write some of the bits and pieces in 1931, much to Walter's disgust and for the 1932 edition James R Gregson was also commissioned to contribute pieces as Walter's output was in decline.

Towards the end of 1931, Walter was found to have cancer. He had been arranging to go with friends to Jerusalem. Even during his last few weeks of life, Walter kept asking his younger daughter, Millicent (Dolly) if she had been to Wakefield to pay for the holiday. The holiday was not to be, for Walter Hampson died in February 1932.

The *Almanack* of 1932 contained a piece by Walter's son Herbert, who also wrote a short biographical sketch of his father (Figure 12). This was supported in the same

Figure 12. The last Almanack to which Hampson contributed.

issue by an appreciation by Sir Ben Turner. Much of the 1932 *Clock* had already been prepared by Walter. The *Almanack* in 1933 was a much thinner volume as the publishers struggled to find writers of quality to take Walter's place.

In 1934 a piece of work surfaced which Walter had been working on for many years, as it had been some time since he had travelled to gather this information. This final work, published in 1934, was *Roomin' i' Rooam, Flirtin' i' Florence, Voyigin' i' Venice.*

Sir Ben Turner put out a subscription list for a suitable memorial for Walter, and in 1935, a memorial tablet listing the incumbents was unveiled in Normanton Parish Church, not far from where Walter Hampson lay buried. The inscription states,

> *1864   In Memory of Walter Hampson   1932*
> *Yorkshire Dialect writer and student of Local History.*

His own poem from *Songs of the Line* can be used to sum up the attitude of life that this quite remarkable railway man had.

> *As th' wheels o' time gooa drivin' rahand,*
> *An' th' yeears pass one bi' one*
> *Eeach yeear passes allus leaves*
> *Some tasks we hevn't done;*
> *An' ivvery day 'at comes an' gooas*
> *Brings sorrow, joy an' strife,*
> *Soa, lets all do us best to try*
> *An' sweeten th' cup o' life.*

Acknowledgments

Most of the information given here has been gained from Walter Hampson's youngest daughter, Millicent, his grand-daughter Dorothy Lau and other relatives. To all I offer my sincere thanks.

Notes and References

1. The stone is on the right of the path going to the church from Church Lane.
2. They both died on the same day.
3. This is from a four verse poem entitled *Gentle Jane*.
4. These were Herbert, Alice, Sydney and Gertrude May.
5. These were Percy and Millicent. Minnie and Edith died when babies. Hampson wrote a poem 'Edith's Grave' published in 1905

> *Here I will plant a daisy white*
> *On little Edith's grave,*
> *'Tis but a simple little flower,*
> *So modest, yet so brave.*

6. The quotation was a comment by Mrs Millicent Jones.
7. James Henry Thomas (1874-1949) General Secretary of N U R, President of T U C, M P for Derby 1910-1931 and many other positions. He was a man of engaging common sense and humour. George Hughes was Chief Engineer for the Lancashire and Yorkshire Railway 1906-1911.
8. This was published by Walter Hampson and was printed by The King's Cross Publishing Co Ltd, London., price 6d. and 1/-.
9. Bryham Kirkby is believed to have been a firm friend and to have accompanied Walter Hampson on many of his excursions, but nobody can now remember how the association was formed.
10. This information can be found in *A Brief History O'T' Owd Clock* by Walter Hampson, 1929.

12. THE STORY OF CROFTON BAND

by Kate Taylor

THE SECOND HALF OF THE NINETEENTH CENTURY saw the formation of many brass bands, often in association with a colliery or other industrial concern. But although the band based at Crofton was, for a period, to be known as the Nostell Colliery Band, it originated rather as a village band and since 1993 has reverted to the name of Crofton Silver Band which it first took in 1936 when instruments changed from brass to silver.

It seems that the band was founded in December 1873. The first references so far found to it lie in the reports in the *Wakefield Herald* and the *Wakefield Express*, both of 17 April 1875, of its playing at the re-opening of Crofton Parish Church following a major restoration. The players gathered in Miss Magnall's schoolroom before parading to the church for services on both the afternoon and evening of 13 April. They also played to entertain those having tea between the services. Their programme included a 'pretty march', the *Big Drum Quickstep*, the *Daisy Dell Quadrille*, the *French Lancers, Auld Lang Syne*, and *Safe in the Arms of Jesus*. The band leader was Joe Stead and the bandmaster for the occasion was Robert Buckle of the fourth West Yorkshire militia.

The rules, laid out in 1912, insisted that members must attend two practices a week but that there must be no practices on Sundays.

Figure 1. Crofton Band passing through the village for the Labour Party carnival in c1950. *Crofton Band archive*

The earliest surviving minute book of the band committee dates from 1911 when it met in Crofton Council School and its chairman was the vicar of Crofton, Reverend H Brownrigg. Its business included getting the band room whitewashed, having the instruments repaired, accepting a tender from the Gas Company to fix a pendant light, admitting new members and arranging a whist drive and dance.

Organising fund-raising events has always been one of the main tasks of the committee. By the 1920s, and perhaps earlier, these included an annual gala or carnival, when there was a procession of floats through the village to the cricket ground. The carnival was revived after the Second World War but was abandoned when the Labour Party instituted its own local galas (Figure 1). Other sources of income have been dances, raffles, beetle drives, coffee evenings sweepstakes, and donations from local benefactors. Major A E Greaves gave a regular donation in the 1940s and 1950s for example. In the past the families at Crofton Hall and Crofton Old Hall (which later became part of Crofton High School) exercised a measure of patronage. Colonel Wilson of Crofton Hall was the band's president for a time. In the 1920s and 1930s the Old Hall was owned by the Hurst family. Both they and the Wilsons would invite the band to play when they were entertaining friends.

Before the First World War the bandroom was at the rear of the *Cock and Crown* public house on Doncaster Road. In the 1920s Joe Castle, a local haulage contractor, rented a small building in the centre of the village to the band for a token £1 a year. When, in 1937, the premises were needed by Mr Castle himself, the band moved to Crofton Working Men's Club. The accommodation there was too small and the landlord of the *Royal Oak*, in the centre of Crofton, agreed to approach the owners, John Smith's Brewery, for permission for the band to use the function room. It was given the room for its practices rent free and with no charge for heating and lighting (Figure 2).

During the Second World War, the army commandeered the band room and, it seems, damaged instruments - some of them irreparably - destroyed early minute books and burned some of the band music that was stored there. Other instruments were stolen during the war years. With the calling-up of younger members, the band effectively dispersed. At the end of hostilities the available players took part in a victory parade and in the armistice day parade in November 1945. That Christmas they set out to raise funds for the band by touring the village. But it was a struggle to keep the band together: some members had not yet been demobilised; others were working on shifts and at weekends. In 1947 Hollingsworth took over the licence at the *Royal Oak* and encouraged the band to re-form. It did and continued to practise at the *Royal Oak* until 1974 when a change of landlord, who gave no support, led to its moving to the upstairs room at Crofton Working Men's Club. The band met there for the next twenty years. Since 1995 the band has again held its twice-weekly practices, on Monday and Thursday evenings, at the *Royal Oak*,

Joe Stead remained the conductor of the band until the early 1900s. By 1925 the bandmaster was Thomas Townend, who had lost his right arm during the First World War and who played the cornet with only one hand. He retired from the band in 1953 and was followed as conductor by Ernest Slinger who stayed for 21 years. Ernest Slinger's son, Mel, joined the band when he was eleven and went on to form his own dance band. Lionel Kirby, who had originally been a guest conductor for appearances at contests, and who was conductor of the Stanley Newmarket band, followed Ernest Slinger. Then a number of bandmasters took over in fairly quick succession, including Roy Bedford, Alan Cross, Brian Dyson and Brian Nicholson. The present conductor, Frank Hoyland, came to the post in 1997.

The band had a significant part in Crofton's Festival of Britain celebrations in August 1951. It played for the open-air service held in the school playground on 2 August and provided a concert in the Parochial Hall the following Wednesday. W Foley was the soloist.

The annual meeting in February 1953 had to face the problem that the band needed twenty-five new instruments, at an estimated cost of £2,500, and that there was a mere £60 in the bank. The meeting decided to open negotiations with a view to obtaining sponsorship by becoming associated with Nostell Colliery. The great majority of bandsmen were at that time employed in the coal industry. The band was renamed Nostell Colliery Band two years later. For a short time committee meetings were held at Nostell Miners' Welfare, in what had been a mission hall and later became a social centre. The change brought little advantage other than that the

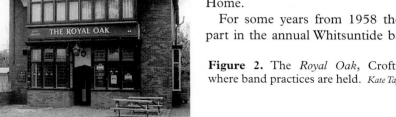

Coal Industry Social and Welfare Organisation (CISWO) provided reconditioned instruments and funded half the cost of new uniforms. For a time the colliery manager was the band's president.

In 1956 the band gave a concert at Nostell Priory to mark the visit of Sir Alec Douglas Home.

For some years from 1958 the band took part in the annual Whitsuntide band contests

Figure 2. The *Royal Oak*, Crofton, where band practices are held. *Kate Taylor.*

Figure 3. As Nostell Colliery Band, the Crofton players taking part in one of the Whitsuntide band contests in Saddleworth in the 1980s. The photograph was taken in Chew Valley Road, Greenfield. *Crofton Band archives*

in Saddleworth (featured in the film *Brassed Off*) see Figure 3. This mammoth event originated in the nineteenth-century Sunday school Whit walks. The walks still take place, on Whit Friday, with villages and towns each forming their own committee, and churches and chapels, sometimes in partnership, hiring bands. The morning is given to hymn-singing and processions led by the bands. In the afternoon there are sporting events and in the evening there are competitions between the bands, held on many different sites simultaneously, with the bands travelling by coach from one to another. The bands are assessed on their marching in the streets as well as their performance in the parks or fields. Such is the popularity of the event that it has spread in the 1990s to Ashton, Mossley, Oldham and Thameside.

In the 1960s the band attended the miners' gala at Seaham, county Durham, and also played from 1947 until the 1980s at Yorkshire miners' demonstrations and galas.

Since 1971 there have been regular exchange visits with the Spielleuteverein Westerbauer band from Hagen, West Germany. These originated after an exchange visit between pupils at Crofton High School and those from a school in Hagen. The German visitors heard the band practising and one of the teachers suggested that the band visit their home town. 1971 saw the band's first visit to Hagen and the following year the Hagen band came to Crofton for the first time. In 1973 it was the fiftieth anniversary of the German band and Crofton players took part in an international band festival in

Germany with 72 members and friends enjoying a ten-day stay. When the Hagen band comes to Crofton some 50 - 60 members stay with the Crofton bandspeople's families and friends. A banner, provided by the Hagen band, is displayed outside the *Royal Oak*, proclaiming the friendship between the two groups. When the German visitors came in August 1998 there was a concert and firework display at Nostell Priory, and concerts by the two bands in Crofton and Sharlston Working Men's Clubs. The Hagen band played in Normanton Park and at Pontefract Racecourse, and they were taken on a trip to York with a visit to Samuel Smith's Brewery. Loyalty, enthusiasm and the strength of local musicianship are all very evident in the length of service of some of the band's members. Arthur Hirst joined it in 1919 at the age of ten and remains a supporter 80 years later. Some Crofton families have provided members over several generations. Harry Thackrah's son Roy and grandson Mark both followed him into the band. So many members of the Foley family belonged to it that at one time it was nicknamed 'Foley Band' (Figure 4). For a period six of them were in the band at the same time. The first to join were the two brothers John and Bill; they were followed by two more brothers Paddy and Mick. Three members of the next generation joined the band, Paddy junior, Mick junior and Noreen, and in 1983 Diane Foley, daughter of Mick junior, joined to play the timpani. Principal cornet player Mick Foley junior, who died early in 1999 had been a member for fifty years. Harold Booth retired in 1998 after 54 years for eighteen of which he was the band's secretary. He became the band's president in 1998. John Roach, who joined the band in 1959, was secretary from 1977

Figure 4. Five members of the Foley family. Left to right: Paddy Foley, Bill Foley, John T Foley MBE, JP, Mick Foley, and Paddy Foley junior. *Crofton Band archive*

Figure 5. Members of the band with some of their trophies won in the early 1980s. From left to right: Harry Thackrah, Brian Nicholson, John Roach and Andrew Schofield. The CISWO trophy is the second from the left. *Crofton Band archive*

to 1995 and is still playing in the band.

In 1993 the band reverted to the name of Crofton Silver Band. Its first engagement under the revived name was at the annual party for Crofton's senior citizens held in the hall of Crofton High School. The first item in the programme was the march, *On the Quarter Deck*, by Kenneth Alford, chosen at the request of H Booth junior because it was the first piece the band had played after it reformed in 1945.

A junior band was formed in May 1995. Training is provided by Roger Hine, Alan Clutten, Colin Slasser and Brian Nicholson. A grant from the Parish Council enabled the purchase of some instruments; others were given or loaned by senior members. Among its engagements in 1998 was a carol concert at Ackworth Methodist Church. A donation from Crofton Parish Council early in 1999 provided the juniors with new uniforms. In 1999 they took part in musical festivals at Pontefract and Rothwell.

In 1997 the band was awarded a lottery grant of £44,668 to enable it to acquire a complete set of new instruments. The band takes part in various competitions, including the Mineworkers National Contest organised by CISWO and supported by RJB Mining. It has to compete with other Yorkshire bands in a regional heat in Sheffield City Hall. Its first taste of the finals was in the 1970s. In 1982 it came first in its section (Figure 5). In December 1995 it came second in its section. In December 1997 it again took part in the finals of the CISWO competition held on 15 November at the Winter Gardens, Blackpool. The test piece for the third section, in which the band was placed, was Aeronauts, by Geoff Richards. Peter Kitson was the

Figure 6. Nostell Colliery (Crofton) band in 1961 at Hammersmith Town Hall after winning fourth prize in its section in the Daily Herald National Band Contest. Lionel Kirby holds the baton. *Crofton Band archive*

conductor for the occasion. The band also competes in the National Brass Band Championships, taking part in the Yorkshire regional heat and - sometimes - getting through to the finals. In 1961, in the period when the *Daily Herald* sponsored the contest, it took fourth prize in its section (Figure 6). It qualified twice more for the finals in the 1960s.

Armistice Day has always been an important event in the band's calendar. In the 1930s it alternated between playing at the service in Crofton and in Walton. In recent years it has played at Pontefract.

There are concerts in Walton Village Hall. At Christmas members of both the junior and senior bands play carols in the village streets and perhaps in places like the Ridings shopping centre in Wakefield and the Asda store at Durkar. They play for a carol concert in Crofton Church.

The start of the band's 125th year was marked by an Anniversary Concert at Crofton High School with guest soloist Jim Shepherd of the Black Dyke Mills Band.

On 28 February 1999 the band qualified in the Yorkshire area heat to play in the finals of the National Brass Bands of Great Britain contest, for the first time in 33 years. The event was at St George's Hall, Bradford. They played *Main Street* and were conducted on the occasion by Peter Kitson.

Acknowledgments

The author is most grateful to Harold Booth, president of the band and long-term member, for his assistance in preparing this account and for allowing her to read his ms history of the band.

Sources

The *Wakefield Express*.
Crofton Smoke Signal.
Michael and Peter Fox, *A Saddleworth Whitsuntide*, 1990.

13. Giving Effect to the Donor's Intentions: Frieston's and Sagar

by Sue Lambert

TO THE CASUAL OBSERVER the two sets of buildings pictured here look unremarkable but their function reveals a charitable legacy going back over four centuries (Figures 1 and 2). They are modern, purpose-built brick dwellings; only discreetly positioned plaques on walls enclosing each group reveal their connections. Each plaque is inscribed with just a few simple details:

Frieston's and Sagar's almshouses, founded 1597,
replaced 1985.
Freeston and Sagar's almshouses
Sagar's Croft,
Walnut Drive,
Normanton
founded 1597, replaced 1997.

Figure 1. Frieston and Sagar's almshouses of 1985. *Sue Lambert.*

Figure 2. Sagar Croft, opened 1997. *Sue Lambert.*

Apart from the fact that the spelling of Frieston varies, this is the first indication that the two charities have been combined.

Historically, the use of plaques to provide details about almshouse charities is fairly common. They are usually positioned in a prominent place on the fabric of the building, such as the main entrance, and are readily seen by people passing by and those entering the building. The original Frieston's almshouse did have a plaque which was recorded by several local antiquaries and commentators. W S Banks in his *Walks about Wakefield*, originally published in 1871, included the following:

> *John Frieston of Altofts, Esq.*
> *Founded and endowed this hospital,*
> *AD 1595. He that have mercy*
> *on the poor happy is he. - Prov 14.21*[1]

In his book of 1862, John Hewitt gave the date as 1591, although he prefaced this with an admission that this was only his recollection of the inscription.[2]

Although it is true that because almshouse plaques were usually exposed to all weather conditions, the lettering could become worn and legibility reduced over a period of several centuries, the discrepancies in date here raise a general point about plaques. As evidence for establishing the foundation date of a charity they are useful and easily accessible, but there are inherent dangers attached to accepting the information given: the date on the plaque could be the date when the actual building was begun, or completed, or when the first almsfolk took up residence, or it could be the date that the endowment was bestowed on the charity. Additional forms of evidence should be taken into consideration, such as the indentures setting up the endowment, and the will of the founder. So, although the plaque on Frieston's Hospital, as recorded by Banks, states that the charity was founded and endowed in 1595, other evidence shows that the endowment was actually established in 1592, John Frieston's will was dated 1594 and the building work on his almshouse began in 1595. It would not be unusual for construction to take a few years and therefore the modern date of 1597 was probably the year when the first inhabitants moved into Frieston's Hospital. It would also be easy to make a quick assumption, from the modern plaques, that the date of 1597 reflects the earlier of the two charities. However other sources show that Sagar's almshouse was founded in 1558!

Originally the two hospital buildings were located quite close to each other. One entry in the Warmfield burial registers even refers to them as the 'Nether and Lower Hospital'.[3] Indeed in relation to the parish church, Sagar's was below the church to the north-east and Frieston's was positioned on higher ground to the south-west.

It was in 1838 when the administration of the two charities was first amalgamated, by a scheme drawn up by the Court of Chancery. Such recourse to the courts was lengthy and costly, but at the time was the only means available to alter the terms of a charity legally. Public concern about the mismanagement of charities in the nineteenth century meant that government responded by establishing a series of commissions with members authorised to travel throughout England and Wales to discover the existence of charitable trusts and note any known abuses connected with them. Reports on the Charity Commissioners' findings were published on a county by county basis. These are extremely useful to the historian and form

> an indispensable work of reference...staggering in bulk and impressive...in detail.[4]

The response of local people to these inquiries was generally welcoming; it was, after all, a chance for them to raise formally their concerns about how local charities were being run. This was certainly the case for Sagar's and Frieston's almshouses. The Commissioners stated that in respect to Frieston's Hospital:

> some of the topics of complaint suggested to us, which were of a trivial nature, were satisfactorily answered...the rest appear to originate partly in a misconception of the nature of the charity and the property destined to its support, and in part, probably, from the notion that the inhabitants of the parishes from whence the almspeople were to be taken have a right of control over the trustees.[5]

Ad hoc inquiries into charities led to the establishment in 1853 of the Charity Commission, which continues to provide a valuable role in registering and monitoring charities today. Further schemes for the Frieston and Sagar's Almshouse Charity were made under the direction of the Commission, including the 1897 scheme by which the charity is currently administered.

Combining Frieston's and Sagar's almhouse charities ensured their continuing existence and certainly the histories of each charity demonstrated several difficulties. The problems were common to many almshouse charities and often stemmed from the restrictions of their foundation deeds, and were further exacerbated by fluctuating economic and demographic circumstances and changing social attitudes over several centuries. The foundation documentation was concerned with the initial setting up of the charity and the provision for the subsequent administration of the almshouse. This included the number of almsfolk to be catered for, any qualifying factors which were to be imposed on potential inhabitants, the form and level of return expected from any endowment which would provide for the future income of the charity, and who the trustees were to be and what their role was in the administration of the charity.

The details used by a founder to distinguish the type of person considered acceptable for a place in the almshouse included age, status, gender, and character of the individual as well as a residential qualification. Just two parishes are represented in the case of Frieston's and Sagar's almshouses: Sagar's almsfolk were to have resided in Warmfield and Frieston's were to be 'elected in turn out of the parishes of Warmfield and Normanton, and not elsewhere.'[6] Significantly these parishes are central to the lives of the founders: Othoneus Sagar was the vicar of Warmfield. John Frieston owned property in Warmfield and lived at Altofts Hall in the parish of Normanton. Both founders were local men.

Those living in Sagar's almshouse could be aged men or women and were to be known as Brother or Sister. Frieston's Hospital was single sex, the seven elderly male inhabitants referred to as Brother. This nomenclature and the use of the term 'hospital', which Sagar also used to describe his almshouse in his will, reflects the medieval origins of almshouses. Although not linked in any way to monastic foundations, both of these sixteenth century charities have retained in their terminology the concept of hospitality, of giving alms and of being separate communities.

There was provision in Frieston's Hospital, in addition to the seven men, for one aged, honest, unmarried woman to be a housekeeper. She was to do the cooking and laundering for the men, and to keep the almshouse clean. She was to be accommodated in a separate house, on land adjoining the hospital. Presumably the founder thought it appropriate to keep the lodgings separate for the sake of propriety and because of her distinct status as housekeeper. This consideration was not given by Sagar because his foundation was a mixed one; any women were present on the same basis as men; separate rooms were provided within the single-storey dwelling. In practice, however, it was often the case that the almsfolk living there

Figure 3. Frieston Hospital, Kirkthorpe. *Sue Lambert*

at any one time were all of the same sex. Frieston's Hospital was also single storeyed; the floorplan was a square, having a large central communal hall with seven smaller rooms opening off it on three sides. The building still survives as a private house and is particularly unusual in its appearance (Figure 3).

Although Frieston's was not a large almshouse foundation, it became difficult to find the full complement of seven men. By the second half of the nineteenth century this difficulty was noted by several observers. When he visited the hospital in 1863 John Hewitt saw only two of the rooms were being used as bedrooms, one by a James Shaw aged 72, the other by another old man who was not present.[7] Similarly when W S Banks visited in 1865 he discovered that only three almsmen were actually living there and four years later there were again just two.[8] Interestingly, Hewitt quoted a conversation with one Joseph Abel who had once been an inhabitant but who had left the hospital to go and live in Wakefield because he 'preferred a jovial and merry life'.[9] This suggests that he, and perhaps others, found the almshouse quiet and rather staid; certainly some restrictions would be placed on inhabitants as they would be required to observe any of the almshouse rules and regulations. Joseph Abel's comment also reflects a change in social attitude; communal living was no longer considered ideal and greater emphasis was placed on privacy. The problem of appointing and retaining almsmen was a major topic raised during the Charity Commissioners' inquiry. The investigation highlighted several dubious management decisions and bad practices that had evolved during the lifetime of the almshouse. At the inquiry

> *'serious complaints were made as to the use of the buildings for other than their legitimate purposes'.*[10]

Rooms had been variously used for the Sunday School and as a venue for parish council meetings, a fact confirmed by Hewitt's visit: 'a number of scholars were then engaged singing some hymns'.[11] So the comment made by a parishioner to the Charity Commissioners was entirely understandable, 'that the almspeople were annoyed by the disturbance'. This was countered by the vicar who said that:

> *the fact was that they were annoyed at having to live in the almshouse at all, and that there was great difficulty in finding aged persons who were willing to become inmates.*[12]

The situation was complicated by the fact that in previous years a practice of almsmen living out had evolved, whereby the men did not reside in the hospital but still received their allowance. This was clearly against the terms of the original rules which made clear that if any inhabitant was absent from the hospital for more than twenty-eight days their allowance was forfeited during that term; the ultimate sanction of expulsion was to be invoked if they failed to return within three months. The Charity Commissioners concluded that

> *the system of a common habitation, such as the Frieston's almshouse, is not appreciated by the class for whom it is designed*

but understood that the trustees were unwilling to abandon the almshouses for the system of outdoor pensions.[13] By the terms of the Charity Commission scheme of 1897 the number of almsfolk was set to four, or if funds permitted, five. The whole issue of outdoor pensioners was a recurring one; by 1898 signed medical certificates were required from non-resident pensioners before they received their allowance.[14]

The decline in numbers inhabiting an almshouse was a common problem and was frequently due to financial pressures. Founders usually left an endowment, generally in the form of a rent on land or property, which was intended to provide an income for the charity in perpetuity. This would be used primarily to provide the almspeople with an allowance for their maintenance, and some founders provided for the surplus being used for repairs to their almshouse. John Frieston endowed his hospital with land at Pontefract while Onotheus Sagar bequeathed land in Castleford. Economic factors meant that charity incomes often fell in real terms and they were particularly vulnerable to inflation over a long period of time. As a result, many almshouse incomes struggled to meet the standard of maintenance intended by the founder. Sagar's almsfolk were to receive three pounds each per year, paid on a quarterly basis. Frieston's almspeople, including the housekeeper, were to be provided with twelve shillings each weekly. But it was not possible for this level to be maintained and by 1865 it had been reduced to only four shillings (20p) The scheme of 1897 attempted to accommodate the effects of inflation by identifying an allowance of not less than six shillings (30p) and not more than ten shillings (50p) weekly.

Remarkably Othoneus Sagar had provided a degree of flexibility for the numbers inhabiting his almshouse. In his will he referred to:

> *so many poor folk as should be assigned...according as the rents should extend to.*[15]

The building was originally constructed to house four poor people, each occupying one room, but by the time of the Charity

Commission's inquiry it had become expedient to reduce the number to two, and as a result each inhabitant had more living space. Unfortunately it seems that there was never a time when the income of the charity recovered sufficiently to restore the number of inhabitants to four; instead any surplus money was diverted to repairs. Already rebuilt in 1766, the location and construction of the building meant that there was a constant battle to keep it in good repair. The Charity Commissioners' report in the nineteenth century found that: 'the roof is not channelled, floors of flagstones laid directly on the soil' and furthermore that the almshouse was built on meadowland which was frequently flooded by the river Calder. As a result, damp was an ongoing problem both in regard to the fabric of the building and to the health of the inhabitants. Improvements were carried out but the trustees made it clear that they were of 'the opinion that the building is still dangerous as a residence for aged people.

John Frieston had made no specific provision for repairs to his hospital and when these were carried out, timber from charity land was sold to finance them. Again the Charity Commission scheme of 1897 rectified the problem, establishing a repair fund. In 1943 a window in Sagar's almshouse had been 'broken by boys with catapults'. It was suggested in 1950 that the two almshouses be rebuilt 'in one comprehensive building' but this was rejected by the Charity Commission. By 1955 Sagar's almshouse was condemned as uninhabitable by the local authority and Frieston's hospital closed in 1967. Permission to sell the latter was granted by the Charity Commission in 1970 and new building commenced on another site in 1983.[16]

Trustees are appointed to be responsible for the management of a charity and providing a continuing succession of appropriate trustees is essential for its proper administration. This might well prove difficult and the problem is particularly well illustrated in just one aspect of almshouse trustees' responsibilities, that of electing almspeople. Othoneus Sagar placed trusteeship firmly in the hands of people in the local community. Those charged with this duty were to be 'four of the most substantial, honest men of the parish'.[17] In contrast John Frieston assigned this duty to the masters of University College, Oxford and Emmanuel College, Cambridge, the rector of Lincoln College, Oxford, one fellow of the former two colleges by them sent for that purpose into Yorkshire, the vicars of Wakefield, Pontefract, Leeds, Normanton and Kirkthorpe, and to his cousin Richard Frieston,

> *or the more part of so many of them as for that purpose should be assembled in the church of Normanton.*[18]

It is a curious assortment of individuals and, considering the cost and time needed for travel, unlikely to be popular among those named; after all, trusteeship is an unpaid duty. Indeed the Charity Commissioners' inquiry found that:

> *none of the trustees appointed by the will, except the vicar of Wakefield, has been in the habit of acting in the management of the charity for many years past.*[19]

Again this roused the suspicion of local inhabitants and certainly did not conform to the founder's intention,. but, like other alterations, it was done for expediency and effectively meant that the charity had continued which it might otherwise not have done. The Charity Commission scheme of 1897 provided for ten trustees, all from the locality. It was a far more appropriate arrangement and local knowledge was reflected in the process of electing almsfolk. In 1902, for example, a man was elected who was

> *considered highly satisfactory in accord with the opinions held by those trustees to whom he is personally known.*[20]

With any charity, the integrity, loyalty and dedication of trustees is essential to their continued survival and success. The example of Frieston's and Sagar's Almshouse Charity has shown that

> *charities were not intended to become quaint museum pieces by the men...who gave their property to help their fellow creatures' and further demonstrates 'the duty of trustees to consider how best to give effect to the donor's intentions in the conditions of today.*[21]

Sagar's Croft, for example, was specifically designed for wheelchair access, a concept undreamed of by the charity's founder.

Acknowledgments

I am very grateful to the clerk to Frieston and Sagar's Almshouse Charity, Mr Kirk, and his wife for their hospitality when I visited them whilst researching the charity.

Notes and References

1. W S Banks, *Walks about Wakefield*, reprint of 1983, p260.
2. J Hewitt, *The Historiography and Topography of the Parish of Wakefield and its Environs*, Vol 1, 1862, p159.
3. W S Banks, *op cit*, p257.
4. D Owen, *English Philanthropy, 1660-1960*, 1965.
5. Reports of those endowments of the Commissioners for inquiry concerning charities, 1818-1837, *Endowed Charities, Administrative County of the West Riding of York*, Vol 4, Eastern and Central Division, 1899, p726.
6. *Ibid*, p720.
7. J Hewitt, *op cit*, p139.
8. W S Banks, *op cit*, p139.
10. Reports on those endowments of the Commissioners for inquiry concerning charities, *op cit*, p733.
11. J Hewitt, *op cit*, p159.
12. Reports of those endowments of the Commissioners for inquiry concerning charities, *op cit*, p733.
13. *Ibid*.
14. Minute book 1897-1996, held by the clerk to Frieston and Sagar's Almshouse Charity.
15. Reports on those endowments of the Commissioners for inquiry concerning charities, *op cit*, p720.
16. Minute book 1897-1996.
17. Reports on those endowments of the Commissioners for inquiry concerning charities, *op cit*, p720.
18. *Ibid*.
19. *Ibid*, p721.
20. Minute book 1897-1996.
21. B Nightingale, *Charities*, 1973, p18.
22. J M Hobson, *Some Early and Later Houses of Pity*, 1926, p183.

14. HOLLIN HALL TRAMWAY, CLIFF COLLIERY AND THE CLIFF COAL AND FIRECLAY COMPANY

by Keith Wainwright

MY INTRODUCTION TO THE OLD HOLLIN HALL TRAMWAY came, I seem to recall, during the school summer holidays of the mid-1950s. I vividly remember my father - who was at that time colliery surveyor at Crigglestone - being called out to investigate yet another surface collapse, this being situated to the rear of the Co-op at Daw Green, Painthorpe. This area was not usually subject to such anomalies, which were of common occurrence in other districts of the parish, more usually at Durkar or Calder Grove where surface collapses into old shallow mineworkings seemed at one time to be a regular feature of everyday life. The collapse at Daw Green posed a dilemma however, in that there was no history of surface collapse or record of the presence of any old shallow mineworkings in the area. There was a possibility that the collapse had been brought about by the deterioration and failure of an old shaft, perhaps one linked with the old fireclay works which had at one time occupied the area.[1] This was not to prove the case however, as a closer inspection on that summer afternoon was ultimately to reveal.

I remember gingerly approaching that recently fenced off area of unstable land close on my father's heels and peering down into the black abyss. Near the base of the collapse and easily recognised amongst the surrounding loose material was the apex of a perfectly formed brick arch, broken only where its failure had provided an ingress for material to enter the tunnel void directly beneath. It was clearly evident that the collapse had not been brought about by the failure of shallow mineworkings or shaft deterioration but by the

Figure 1. Hollin Hall tramway, Daw Green to Broad Cut.

deterioration and ultimate failure of an underground tunnel, later to be confirmed as that which carried the old Hollin Hall tramway beneath Little Cliff at Crigglestone.[2] Though there are few physical reminders of the old tramway visible today, ample documentary evidence of its route does exist as do limited details of its construction (Figure 1).[3] The surviving evidence enables us to examine in more detail this notable engineering achievement.

Before studying in more detail the requirement for the construction of the tramway however, the desirability for its construction relative to the history of the Crigglestone coalfield should first be established. There are many references to Crigglestone coal and its colliers in the surviving manor court rolls. Probably the first comes from the roll of 1316, where reference is made to the illegal removal of coal by Robert, son of Hugh de Chapelthorp from 'shallow ditches' dug on the lord of the manor's land.[4] From those early years of surface or outcrop workings, mining activities flourished in the parish, and evidence of early working by bell pit methods has been unearthed by more recent opencast mining operations in the Durkar, Hall Green and Hollingthorpe districts.[5] Ventures into deeper mining in Crigglestone were modestly pursued when suitable methods of ventilation and drainage became available. Workings from this eighteenth century period have been discovered in the parish, being particularly evident in the Newmillerdam and Woolley Moor districts.[6] The first successful underground mining operations of any consequence appear to have been those undertaken by Joseph Charlesworth beneath his Hollin Hall estate at Dirtcar between 1795 and 1812.[7] These relatively shallow workings in the Beamshaw seam have been 'breached' over the years by later workings and have, as previously stated, been the subject of numerous surface collapses.

The workings of Joseph Charlesworth were situated in close proximity to the Upper Calder Navigation at Dirtcar. The Navigation, which had been completed in 1762, gave him ease of access to transport along the inland waterway system and alleviated many of the problems other colliery owners were facing in the distribution of coal from the pit head.[8] There is reference to Hollin Hall coal wagons being used in 1807.[9] These are said to have had a capacity of 42 cwt., and may have been horse or oxen drawn, probably over a tramway to loading staithes on ·the Navigation at Broad Cut.

Following the exhaustion of coal in the Beamshaw seam under his Hollin Hall estate, Joseph Charlesworth's mining activities were

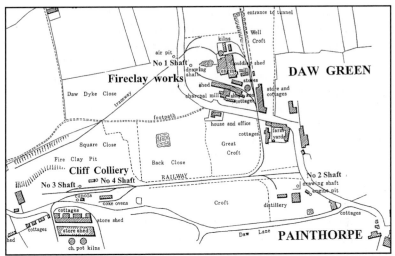

Figure 2. Cliff Colliery, fireclay works and Hollin Hall tramway, 1849.

transferred south of the village to Chapelthorpe and to Woodmoor at Newmillerdam.[10] At Newmillerdam, his family mining concern was to successfully extract coal from the Woodmoor and Winter seams until late into the nineteenth century. By the mid-19th century, major mining activities were also being undertaken at Painthorpe where several workable seams of coal had been proved in the Daw Green district.[11] These seams and their relevant depths were verified in an exploratory borehole sunk on the Cliff estate at Daw Green in 1829.[12] This, sunk to a depth of approximately 150 yards, had passed through the horizons of five coal seams of thicknesses varying from 17 to 40 inches. Three of the seams - the Woodmoor, Winter and Beamshaw were being successfully extracted at many of the small collieries operating in the parish at the time.[13] The trial borehole also proved the existence of shallow beds of fireclay and ganister, both of which were to be worked on the Cliff estate in future years.

The first shafts on the Cliff estate were sunk by owners Robert Marriott, John Philpott and coalmaster Benjamin Burrell at Daw Green between the years 1839 and 1842.[14] By 1842, only modest amounts of coal were being extracted in the Woodmoor seam from the shafts sunk on their estate. Unfortunately for the owners, the potential of the coalfield had not been fully realised.

Determination, a good knowledge of mining and primarily capital were major requirements necessary to exploit the full potential of the colliery at Daw Green. These attributes were readily available to new owners Richard and John Buckingham Pope who acquired the Cliff estate in November 1842.[15] The first priority of the new owners was to increase coal production, an undertaking only achievable by the sinking of new and the deepening of existing shafts to the Winter seam, some 33 yards below the Woodmoor seam horizon.[16] In early 1843, two of the existing shafts, Nos 1 and 2 had been excavated to the Winter Seam level (Figure 2). This allowed coal in both the Woodmoor and Winter Seams to be worked simultaneously. In a period of just over three months, coal production at the colliery had been almost doubled.[17] To alleviate some of the winding, ventilation and pumping problems (the Woodmoor and Winter Seams were both prone to heavy water ingress) which increased production had created, two new shaft sinkings, Nos 3 and 4 were excavated adjacent to Daw Lane at Painthorpe (Figure 3). Both shafts were sunk to the Winter Seam level.[18] These shafts were to become the new upcast and downcast shafts for the colliery, which then became known as Cliff Colliery (see Fig 2).

The exploratory borehole which had been sunk on the Cliff estate in 1829 had proved the existence of shallow fireclay (thickness 48″) and ganister (thickness 19″) deposits in the district. Analysis tests showed that its composition was ideally suited for both brickmaking and pottery purposes.[19] Ganister is the prime requisite for the production of superior quality firebricks and furnace ware. The shallow depth of both fireclay and ganister beds at Painthorpe would make their extraction by quarrying methods a reasonably uncomplicated operation. Richard and John Buckingham Pope, not slow to realise the implications of the findings of the 1829 borehole investigation, were keen to exploit the opportunity the fireclay and ganister deposits afforded them and in 1843 they undertook to erect a clayware manufactory at Daw Green (see Fig 2). Fireclay and ganister were transported to the manufactory by overland tramway from a claypit situated at the rear of the company's Cliff Colliery site. The importance of the clayware manufactory is reflected in the parish register of the period, this showing an influx of skilled workers

Figure 3. Cliff Colliery No 3 upcast shaft, exposed during reclamation work in 1973. *K Wainwright.*

into the district from Stoke and the Staffordshire pottery towns.[21]

To accommodate the increasing numbers of their workforce, cottages were erected by the proprietors in Daw Green, Dennington and Painthorpe and to provide for the educational well being of their employees children, a small school was erected at Daw Green.

The availability of both fireclay and ganister on the estate greatly increased the category of products which could be manufactured there (Figure 4). These products included :

Common bricks
Flue lining and furnace bricks
White pressed bricks
Sanitary clay pipes
Chimney pots
Ridge and pantiles
Terra cotta ornaments and ware.[22]

In late 1843, the mounting problems of coal distribution from the Cliff Colliery pithead and the supply and distribution of finished clayware from the manufactory at Daw Green were causing formidable problems. Under the original owners, coal was carted from the pithead and distributed by means of the vastly inadequate local highway system. Under the ownership of Richard and John Buckingham Pope however, coal production had increased significantly, indeed, it had almost doubled with the introduction of two-seam working at their colliery. Markets were opening up throughout the country, especially the lucrative London market where there was always a ready demand for good quality household coals such as the Woodmoor and bright burning Winter beds. Unrestricted cartage was also required for the concern's clayware products and it was clearly evident that unless an alternative form of transport and distribution for both commodities could be found, the efficient delivery of their products would become severely restricted.

The closest and perhaps the cheapest form of transport available to the firm was by water, the owners having a fleet of over twenty Yorkshire keels at their disposal.[23] The nearest navigable waterway, the Calder and Hebble Navigation, passed through Broad Cut at Dirtcar, some one and a half miles north of the work's Painthorpe

Figure 4. Invoice of the Fireclay Company, 1887.

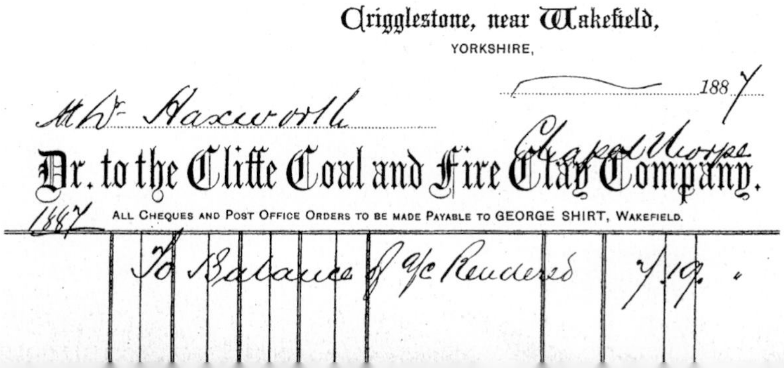

Crigglestone, near Wakefield,

YORKSHIRE,

_____ 188_

Mr. Haxworth

Dr. to the Cliffe Coal and Fire Clay Company.

ALL CHEQUES AND POST OFFICE ORDERS TO BE MADE PAYABLE TO GEORGE SHIRT, WAKEFIELD.

To Balance of a/c Rendered   7/19

location.[24] Work had begun on this navigation at Wakefield in about 1760 and by the early 1770s it had been completed upstream to Sowerby Bridge.[25] Much of the navigation utilised the route of the River Calder, locks being constructed to by-pass the old river weirs. Additional works in the 1830s had improved sections of the canal between Dirtcar and Horbury and under this scheme, a new section of canal had been constructed west of Broad Cut.[26] Until the 1880s, barge horses crossed the River Calder by wooden bridge at Broad Cut to access the Horbury section of the canal (see Figure 1).[27] In the early 1880s, the bridge over the river was washed away in a storm and was never replaced. From that time, horses were ferried across the river to Broad Cut coal staithe by means of flat bottomed boat (Figure 5). It is possible, as has already been noted, that a coal staithe existed at Broad Cut and was used by Joseph Charlesworth as early as 1807 to embark his coal to river vessels from his Hollin Hall coalfield.[28] It was to this point behind Broad Cut Farm and possibly to the staithe previously constructed by Joseph Charlesworth, that Richard and John Buckingham Pope decided to construct an overland tramway from their works at Painthorpe (Figure 6).

By November 1843, wayleaves and leases were being negotiated with landowners along the proposed tramway route and the engineering aspects of its construction were being finalised.[29] The tramway was to be iron framed on sleepers.[30] Between Little Cliff and the Denby Dale turnpike road it was to be self-activating, loaded wagons passing down the incline from Painthorpe hauling empty wagons back up to the works. This operation required the provision of a brake wheel on the summit of the incline connected by wire rope to pulleys along its route. From the turnpike road to the coal staithe at Broad Cut, the wagons were hauled by horses and possibly by oxen. Stables and a smithy situated near the end of the tramway were provided for the wellbeing of the animals.[31] The self-activating single-track tramway system required the provision of a mid-route passing loop, a feature unfortunately omitted from the relevant Ordnance Survey publication of the period. It is probably safe to assume that

Figure 5. The barge horse ferry at Broad Cut, 1932. Broad Cut coal staithe is just visible in the background, right of centre. *C Land.*

Figure 6. Broad Cut Farm, Durkar, 1999. *K Wainwright.*

this loop was situated at mid-distance on the incline and possibly in close proximity to where the tramway passed adjacent to Hollin Hall.

The haulage operation on the tramway was assisted in no small measure by the natural lie of the land. From the works to the Denby Dale turnpike road this decreased in altitude by some 170 feet, and gave an average gradient of almost 1 in 25 along the route of the tramway. To maintain this gradient, a tunnel approximately 250 yards in length had to be driven beneath Little Cliff (Figure 7).[32] This operation was rendered difficult in that it had to be driven on the curve, this being necessary to avoid passing beneath the ancient Manor House Farmstead at Little Cliff. The tramway crossed two highways on its route from the works at Painthorpe to the coal staithe at Broad Cut. These were Hollin Hall Lane and the Denby Dale turnpike at Dirtcar. At Hollin Hall Lane the highway was carried across the tramway by means of a wooden trestle bridge and at Dirtcar an ungated crossing was installed to cross the turnpike. The Hollin Hall tramway (so named because of its proximity to the ancient farmstead of Hollin Hall) was completed and in use by late 1845.[33] From that time, coal and manufactured goods had uninterrupted access from the company's works at Painthorpe directly onto the Calder and Hebble Navigation at Broad Cut.

The majority of the coal, especially the popular bright burning Winter seam, found its way over the inland waterway system and thence by sea to London, where Richard and John Buckingham Pope maintained a business interest at Abbey Wharf, Westminster.[34] The excellent quality clayware products found ready markets both locally and further afield, the firm's keels being used to distribute them both up and down stream from their Broad Cut riverside staithe.

In the late 1840s, the coal industry entered a period of severe depression, and with a need to rationalise their mining interests, and no doubt to concentrate on their other mining activities in the area, Richard and John Buckingham Pope were obliged to put their Cliff estate on the market. In June 1849, it was purchased by John Vickery Broughton of London for £23,050.[35] With ever dwindling reserves of coal in the Woodmoor and Winter seams, - a situation which had probably not escaped the notice of the previous owners, it had become a matter of paramount importance that the new proprietors locate further coal reserves. The decision was taken to deepen No. 3 and No. 4 shafts at Cliff Colliery to the horizon of the Beamshaw seam situated some 27 yards below the Winter bed.[36] By early 1850, coal was being wound from this seam at the colliery and future prospects for the new owners appeared relatively secure. Preliminary experiments conducted on the Beamshaw seam coal showed it to be a capable coking coal, the seam possessing coke producing qualities which had been lacking in both Woodmoor and Winter seams.[37] Coke produced a greater overall heat than coal, and used in the kilns it produced a better quality firebrick. To take full advantage of the process, the proprietors enterprisingly erected a batch of twelve coke ovens adjacent to their Cliff Colliery at Painthorpe (see Figure 2).[38]

As a consequence of coke production, numerous by-products are produced. Pitch, tar, creosote and naptha were three which the firm were able to exploit and for which they were able to find a ready local market. With the erection of coke ovens, distillery, naptha refinery and storage tanks, the area around Cliff Colliery at Painthorpe took on the appearance of a chemical works. The area became known locally as 'the chemic', a name still in use to the present day. The layout of the colliery and manufactory at this time is shown on Figure 2.

The unfortunate death of John Vickery Broughton soon after his

Figure 7. Hollin Hall tramway, Little Cliff tunnel, and Hollin Hall, 1849.

acquisition of the estate was to place a heavy burden on his wife, Anne. It was a responsibility she appears to have tackled successfully during the ensuing ten years with, no doubt, capable assistance from her faithful works manager, George Shirt.

In 1860, the works and colliery again required an extensive investment of capital. Two of the pottery kilns needed urgent attention and the pumping and winding engines at Cliff Colliery - which had been acquired 'second hand' almost 20 years previously, required immediate replacement.[39] The investment was not one which the Broughtons were willing to underwrite and the manufactory and colliery were put on the market. For three years, management of the works and colliery passed into the hands of Samuel Radcliffe Carrington, a Stockport business man and James Fawcett, a Wakefield corn miller. During this period, the major innovation undertaken by the owners was undoubtedly the physical removal of the clayworks manufactory from its original site in Daw Green to an area in the immediate vicinity of the firm, Cliff Colliery at Daw Lane in Painthorpe.[40] Replacement pumping and winding engines were installed at Cliff Colliery and new pottery kilns were erected adjacent to the colliery site to replace the originals, the condition of which was deteriorating rapidly. In 1863, and after only three years of administering the enterprise, the partnership of Samuel Carrington and James Fawcett was dissolved and the estate put up for sale (Figure 8). In 1864 it was purchased by Wakefield corn factor Robert Jefferson Mackie.[42] Mackie was a staunch Liberal and firmly dedicated Methodist. His marriage to a Miss Bownas of York had been blessed with two daughters and four surviving sons - Robert Bownas, Edward Alexander, David and John.

Following the acquisition of the estate by Robert Jefferson Mackie, a partnership agreement was executed.[43] This named the partners as Robert Bownas Mackie, corn factor of Wakefield; David Mackie, gentleman; James Fawcett, corn miller and former partner of Samuel Carrington, and

Figure 8. Cliff Estate sale particulars, 1863.

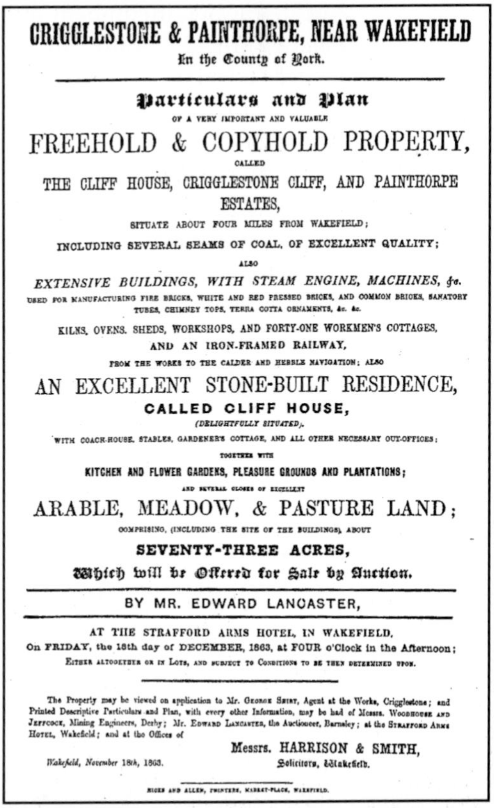

CRIGGLESTONE & PAINTHORPE, NEAR WAKEFIELD

In the County of York.

Particulars and Plan

OF A VERY IMPORTANT AND VALUABLE

FREEHOLD & COPYHOLD PROPERTY,

CALLED

THE CLIFF HOUSE, CRIGGLESTONE CLIFF, AND PAINTHORPE ESTATES,

SITUATE ABOUT FOUR MILES FROM WAKEFIELD;

INCLUDING SEVERAL SEAMS OF COAL, OF EXCELLENT QUALITY;

ALSO

EXTENSIVE BUILDINGS, WITH STEAM ENGINE, MACHINES, &c.

USED FOR MANUFACTURING FIRE BRICKS, WHITE AND RED PRESSED BRICKS, AND COMMON BRICKS, SANATORY TUBES, CHIMNEY TOPS, TERRA COTTA ORNAMENTS, &c. &c.

KILNS, OVENS, SHEDS, WORKSHOPS, AND FORTY-ONE WORKMEN'S COTTAGES,

AND AN IRON-FRAMED RAILWAY,

FROM THE WORKS TO THE CALDER AND HEBBLE NAVIGATION; ALSO

AN EXCELLENT STONE-BUILT RESIDENCE,

CALLED CLIFF HOUSE,

(DELIGHTFULLY SITUATED),

WITH COACH-HOUSE, STABLES, GARDENER'S COTTAGE, AND ALL OTHER NECESSARY OUT-OFFICES;

TOGETHER WITH

KITCHEN AND FLOWER GARDENS, PLEASURE GROUNDS AND PLANTATIONS;

AND SEVERAL CLOSES OF EXCELLENT

ARABLE, MEADOW, & PASTURE LAND;

COMPRISING, (INCLUDING THE SITE OF THE BUILDINGS), ABOUT

SEVENTY-THREE ACRES,

Which will be Offered for Sale by Auction.

BY MR. EDWARD LANCASTER,

AT THE STRAFFORD ARMS HOTEL, IN WAKEFIELD,

On FRIDAY, the 18th day of DECEMBER, 1863, at FOUR o'Clock in the Afternoon;

EITHER ALTOGETHER OR IN LOTS, AND SUBJECT TO CONDITIONS TO BE THEN DETERMINED UPON.

The Property may be viewed on application to Mr. GEORGE SHIRT, Agent at the Works, Crigglestone; and Printed Descriptive Particulars and Plan, with every other Information, may be had of Messrs. WOODHOUSE AND JEFFCOCK, Mining Engineers, Derby; Mr. EDWARD LANCASTER, the Auctioneer, Barnsley; at the STRAFFORD ARMS HOTEL, Wakefield; and at the Offices of

Messrs. HARRISON & SMITH,

Wakefield, November 18th, 1863.   Solicitors, Wakefield.

RIGGS AND ALLEN, PRINTERS, MARKET-PLACE, WAKEFIELD.

George Shirt of Crigglestone, who was also empowered to act as agent for the company, thus occupying a position he had enjoyed in previous years. The newly formed company became known as the Cliff Coal and Fire Clay Company (see Figure 4)

During the following months, the partners carried out a thorough review of their company and its assets. Amongst the radical changes it instigated was to increase the production at their clayware manufactory, reconstructed by Carrington and Fawcett at Daw Lane in the early 1860s. The Hollin Hall tramway still handled the bulk of the company's products, but the sheer volume of materials to be carried to Broad Cut had highlighted the many inadequacies the tramway had, problems which were not to be solved until the company acquired access to the Barnsley branch of the Lancashire and Yorkshire Railway at Dennington in 1871. One other problem, and one which had troubled previous owners in the past was that of dwindling coal reserves. Coal had been extracted from the Beamshaw Seam at Cliff Colliery since 1850.[44] In 1864, reserves only existed in that seam for a further two years' extraction; at that time, coal in all the accessible seams available to the company would have become exhausted. With one exception, all available coal under the land of adjoining property owners had been extracted or was under lease to other parties for extraction. The exception was the coal lying beneath the Painthorpe House estate of the Reverend John Heaton Micklethwaite, incumbent of the parish living of St James Church at Chapelthorpe. Following negotiations in 1867, a lease was formalised between the company and John Micklethwaite granting the company working rights in the Woodmoor, Winter and Beamshaw seams of coal beneath the Painthorpe House estate, the company paying a royalty for the coal extracted.[45] To gain access to the newly acquired coal reserves, the sinking of two new shafts was necessary. These were ultimately completed by the company in 1868 adjacent to the old lane which ran from Painthorpe to Hollingthorpe.[46]

The new colliery, which became known as Hollingthorpe Colliery commenced production in the Woodmoor and Winter seams by the end of 1868 (Figure 9).

Towards the end of 1867, the company was presented with problems it had with astute management previously been able to avoid, when a small group of miners, all members of the West Yorkshire Miners' Association took strike action.[47] Their grievance, they claimed, was against the non payment of an increase in wages they had supposedly negotiated the previous November. The strike lasted for eighteen weeks and ended in defeat for the miners.

1868 saw the closure of the company's Cliff Colliery, the abandonment taking place when reserves in the Beamshaw seam had become exhausted.[48]

In 1850, the Lancashire and Yorkshire Railway Company had opened a branch line from their main Calder Valley line at Horbury Junction through to Barnsley.[49] This line passed through Dennington and within half a mile of the company's colliery and works. A connecting spur to the Barnsley branch at Dennington would serve to alleviate many of the distribution problems which had handicapped the company over the years. The rail link was an expensive option the company had previously contemplated but never seriously considered. By 1870, it had become a necessity. Following amicable negotiations with adjoining landowner Wentworth Blackett Beaumont, a lease signed by the parties in May 1871 granted the coal and fireclay company authorisation to construct a mineral railway from their works and colliery at Painthorpe to what was to become the company's railhead on the L & Y Barnsley branch at Dennington.[50] The new rail link was not completed without engineering difficulties. These included the construction of a section of track at a severe gradient of 1 in 30, and the erection of a 'mini' viaduct on brick piers at the rear of the *Station Hotel* at Dennington.[51] The line was completed by the end of August 1871. In September, the company received delivery of the first of two locomotives it was to purchase from Hudswell Clarke of Leeds.[52] This, an 0-6-0 saddletank with 2' 9" driving wheels, (manufacturers loco No 113), was put to work immediately by the company.

On the completion of the new rail link to Dennington, the company had no further requirement for the old Hollin Hall tramway . The old line which had served the company so well over the years was duly abandoned. A section of the tramway was to receive a reprieve however, and use was found over its lower section from Denby Dale Road to Broad Cut staithe by Thomas Firth, colliery owner at Dirtcar who utilised that section of the tramway until the abandonment of his Dirtcar Colliery in 1878 (Figure 10).[53]

Satisfactory amounts of coal continued to be produced at the company's Hollingthorpe Colliery during the ensuing years, though problems were occasionally encountered in areas of underground faulting and this sometimes severely affected coal production. In an attempt to avoid a district of severely faulted ground, the company sank a third shaft at Hollingthorpe, some 150 yards south of their main shaft complex.[54] New screens were erected adjacent to the new

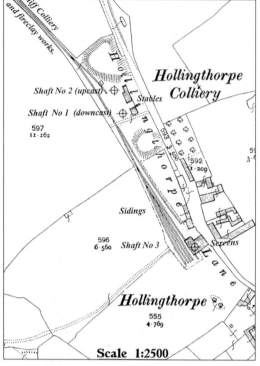

Hollingthorpe Colliery

Shaft No 2 (upcast) ⊕

Stables

Shaft No 1 (downcast) ⊕

597
11·162

592
1·209

Sidings

596
6·560   Shaft No 3

Screens

Hollingthorpe

555
4·769

Scale 1:2500

Figure 9. Hollingthorpe Colliery,
abandoned in 1887.

shaft and the existing mineral railway with extra siding provision was extended to the new sinking (see Figure 9). Production figures for Hollingthorpe Colliery between 1 July 1880 and 30 April 1881, the only known surviving for the colliery, show that it produced 43,019 tons of coal at a value of £11,825 5s 5d during that period.[55] Of this production, 5,444 tons were transferred to the clayware manufactory adjacent. The remainder found its way over the new rail link for dispersal from the company's rail head at Dennington.

In 1884, the company's coal reserves in the Woodmoor and Winter seams at Hollingthorpe were rapidly becoming exhausted. Fortunately they had reserved working rights in the Beamshaw seam under the Micklethwaite lease of 1867. The Beamshaw seam horizon was a mere 27 yards below the level of the Winter bed at Hollingthorpe and accessibility did not on the outset appear to pose any serious problems.[56] Work began immediately on deepening the shafts. There were to be serious problems from the outset of the scheme however, water finding its way down into the shaft sinking from the shallower Woodmoor and Winter shaft insets. The water problems were alleviated to some extent by the installation of underground pumps. These worked continually to allow reasonable working conditions to be maintained during the shaft sinking. Eventually, with the shaft reaching the Beamshaw seam level, extraction commenced in November 1884.[57]

In May 1885, the colliery workings at Hollingthorpe penetrated an area of extensive underground faulting. This allowed excessive amounts of water to enter the Beamshaw seam workings. Serious efforts to keep floodwater levels within reasonable working limits were made by the company but the ingress of water proved to be in excess of the capability of the pumps. New headings were driven on

RAILWAY TRUCKS LOADED AT CRIGGLESTONE STATION,

L. AND Y. RAILWAY.

BOATS LOADED AT HOLLINGHALL STAITH, ROAD &c.

FROM

THOS. FIRTH & CO.,

DIRTCAR COLLIERY,

POST OFFICE ORDERS AND TELEGRAMS
TO WAKEFIELD.   *Nr. WAKEFIELD.*

Figure 10. Letterhead of Thomas Firth & Co, Dirtcar Colliery, 1878.

the rise side of the Beamshaw seam in an attempt to open up a new underground district but unfortunately in May 1886, these headings also penetrated waterlogged faulty ground, the ingress of water completely flooding the pit bottom. There was no alternative open to the company but to abandon the colliery.[58]

The closure of their Hollingthorpe Colliery in May 1886 was to sound the death knell for the company's fireclay works at Painthorpe, the company being totally reliant on the adjacent colliery for its regular fuel supplies. When coal stocks became exhausted in late 1887, the fireclay works closed.[59]

During the subsequent years, several attempts were made to dispose of the fireclay works but it appeared that the lack of a reliable local coal supply made prospective purchasers wary of any capital commitment. In 1891, with no purchaser to hand, the demolition of the works commenced. Within a short period of time, all that remained of the manufactory were the old workshops, offices, claypit and the old furnace chimney on Daw Lane (Figure 11).[60] This chimney, 195 feet high and 60 feet in circumference at its base, became affectionately known by the locals as 'chemic chimney'. Proving stubborn to the end, it was demolished amidst much local publicity in December 1948.[61] In February 1892, 57 workmen's cottages situated at Daw Green, Dennington and Painthorpe came under the auctioneer's hammer at the *Great Bull Hotel* in Wakefield.[62] Many of these properties, the majority of which have survived to the present, were purchased by individuals who had been long time tenants of the company. Other properties were sold en-bloc, complete with sitting tenants. All were constructed in

Figure 11.
Chemic chimney, Painthorpe, shortly before its demolition in 1948. *K Wainwright.*

Figure 12. The remains of Broad Cut coal staithe, June 1965. *K Wainwright.*

brick manufactured at Painthorpe.

Apart from the original company housing referred to above, there are few available reminders of the once thriving industry which so dominated this little corner of the parish. Occasionally, development work in the district might expose the odd reminder of our industrial past as in 1973, when old Cliff Colliery No 3 upcast shaft was uncovered during reclamation work on Daw Lane (see Figure 3). Modern surface development and opencast mining have obliterated much of the physical evidence of Richard and John Pope's Hollin Hall tramway. Until quite recently, the massive oak timber baulks could be seen on the old river side staithe at Broad Cut (Figure 12) but even this structure has now being overtaken by the ravages of time. A brick-built tramway bridge survives in part at the rear of Broad Cut Farm, this perhaps a final memorial to Richard and John Buckingham Pope's local engineering endeavours (Figure 13). With the passing of the old fireclay works at Painthorpe, it was left to the adjoining colliery complex at Woollen Well Main, sunk about 1870 (later to become known as Crigglestone Colliery) to take over the mantle as major employer in the parish, a situation it was to enjoy until its eventual closure in 1968.

Notes and References

1. Six inch OS survey of 1849, sheet 248.
2. Earliest OS editions and early legal documents omitted the 'e' and this form of spelling has been adopted in this historical article.
3. Six inch OS survey of 1849, sheet 248.

Figure 13. The remains of the old tramway bridge at the rear of Broad Cut Farm, Durkar, February 1999. *K Wainwright.*

4. Wakefield Manor Court Rolls, roll of 1316, YAS Record Series Vol 78, Court Rolls Manor of Wakefield, vol 4.
5. Crigglestone Colliery archive, in author's possession.
6. Newmillerdam Colliery archive, in author's possession
7. Crigglestone Colliery archive.
8. The Calder and Hebble Navigation minute books.
9. BTACN.
10. Crigglestone and Newmillerdam Colliery archive.
11. Green's Geological Memoirs, Crigglestone district, 1878.
12. Cliff Estate sale particulars, 1841, in author's possession.
13. Crigglestone Colliery archive.
14. Cliff Estate sale particulars, 1841, in author's possession.
15. West Yorkshire Archive Service, Wakefield.
16. Mine records abandonment plan nos GCR 306/307, Bretby, Staffs.
17. Crigglestone Colliery archive.
18. Mine records abandonment plan no GCR 316, Bretby, Staffs.
19. Geology of the Country around Wakefield, HMSO, 1940.
20. Crigglestone Colliery archive.
21. St James's Church, Chapelthorpe, parish register, West Yorkshire Archives, Wakefield.
22. Cliff Estate sale particulars, 1841.
23. John Goodchild, Pope and Pearson and Silkstone Buildings, 1977.
24. Name changed to Durkar in 1905. Crigglestone Parish Council minute book.
25. Guide to the Calder and Hebble Navigation, 1968.
26. Ibid.
27. 6" OS survey of 1849, sheet 248.
28. John Goodchild, The Coal Kings of Yorkshire, 1978.
29. Agreement, trustees of the late John Moore of Dirtcar House and Richard and John Buckingham Pope of Cliff House, 11 November 1843, the John Goodchild Collection, Wakefield.
30. Cliff Estate sale particulars, 1859, in author's possession.
31 Author's family records.
32. 6" OS survey of 1849, sheet 248.
33. Crigglestone Colliery archive.
34. John Goodchild, Pope and Pearson and Silkstone Buildings, 1977.
35. Ibid.
36. W H Wilcockson, Sections of Strata of Coal Measures of the Yorkshire Coalfield, 1950, Crigglestone Colliery shaft section.
37. Crigglestone Colliery archive.
38. Cliff Estate sale particulars, 1859.
39. Crigglestone Colliery archive.
40. Mine records abandonment plan, No GCR 308, Bretby, Staffs.
41. Cliff Estate sale particulars, 1863, the John Goodchild Collection, Wakefield.
42. West Yorkshire Archives, Wakefield.
43. Crigglestone Colliery archive.
44. Mine records abandonment plan, No GCR 315, Bretby, Staffs.
45. Minerals lease, John Heaton Micklethwait and Robert Bownas Mackie and partners, 1867, the John Goodchild Collection, Wakefield.
46. Crigglestone Colliery archive.
47. F Machin, The Yorkshire Miners, 1958.
48. Mine Records Office, Bretby, Staffs.
49. David Joy, Regional Railway History, Vol 8, 1984.
50. Lease, Wentworth Blackett Beaumont and the Cliff Coal and Fireclay Co, Crigglestone Colliery archive.
51. 1/2500 OS sheet 262/2, 1891.
52. Armley Industrial Museum, Armley, Leeds.
53. Mine records abandonment plan Nos GCR 301, 302, 312, 313, Bretby, Staffs.
54. Mine records abandonment plan No 1878, Bretby, Staffs.
55. Crigglestone Colliery archive.
56. Mine records abandonment plan No 1878, Bretby, Staffs.
57. Crigglestone Colliery archive.
58. Mine records abandonment plan No 1878, Bretby, Staffs.
59. Crigglestone Colliery archive.
60. 1/2500 OS sheet 262/2, 1891.
61. Crigglestone Colliery archive.
62. Cliff Estate sale particulars, 26 February 1892, in author's possession.

CONTRIBUTORS

---

1. WAKEFIELD BY GASLIGHT

Following four and a half years' war service with the Royal Navy, **K O M Golisti** was employed in the gas industry on civil engineering projects, retiring as Pipelines Engineer for the North Eastern Region of the British Gas Corporation. In retirement his objective is to complete an anthology and essays entitled '*The Gas Adventure*' on those undertakings that comprised the Yorkshire gas industry the heritage of which is rapidly slipping into oblivion.

---

2. WAKEFIELD'S SIGNIFICANCE TO A WIDER WORLD
7. DYEING FOR WAKEFIELD: THE STORY OF THE BELLE ISLE DYEWORKS

John Goodchild is a native of Wakefield and was educated at the Grammar School there. He has been active in local historical research since about the age of thirteen, and is the author of over 140 books and published essays on aspects of the history of the West Riding. He was founder-curator of Cusworth Hall Museum and subsequently Archivist to Wakefield MDC; in his retirement he runs a Local History Study Centre which houses his immense collection of manuscripts and research materials, and which is open to use, free of charge, by appointment. Mr Goodchild holds an honorary M Univ from the Open University, awarded for academic and scholarly distinction and for public services. He is a regular contributor to the *Aspects* series. Outside historical research, his interests lie in Freemasonry and in Unitarianism - and his dog.

---

3. OSSETT AND THE GREAT WAR

David Scriven moved to Yorkshire, where he now teaches history at Batley Grammar School, after studying at the University College of Wales, Aberystwyth. He has been interested in local history for more than twenty years and is a founder member of the Ossett Local History Society. He has carried out research on the social and economic development of Ossett in the nineteenth century and has given numerous talks on the subject as well as having an article published in *Old West Riding*.

4. In Place of the Stork: Maternity Provision in Wakefield
12. Brassed On: The Story of Crofton Band

Coral 'Kate' Taylor was born in Wakefield in 1933 and educated at the Girls' High School before going on to St Anne's College, Oxford, where she read English Language and Literature. After teaching in Leeds, at West Park C S School and the City of Leeds and Carnegie College of Education, she took up a post as Principal Lecturer in English at Wentworth Castle College, Stainborough. Following the closure of the College she became Vice-Principal (Community) at Barnsley Sixth Form College when it opened in 1979. Since her retirement in 1990 she has spent her time researching local history. Her book, *Right Royal: Wakefield Theatre 1776-1994* was published in 1995. She works part-time as a tutor for the Open University and is the Hon Managing Editor of Wakefield Historical Publications, President of Wakefield HIstorical Society and Chair of the Mercia Cinema Society.

5. Portobello - Wakefield's First Major Council Housing Scheme

Angela Petyt was born in Wakefield in 1971 and educated at Thornes House School. She gained a BA (Hons) degree in History and Linguistics from the University College of Ripon and York St John. She is now employed as a lecturer in family and local history by the WEA and Thomas Danby College, as well as running her own Heritage Services business specialising in palaeography and the repair of documents and photographs. She will soon commence an Open University course *Studying Family and Community History* (DA301). Angela is currently chairman of the Wakefield and District Family History Society. Her interests include industrial history, archaeology, information technology, music and travel.

6. Wakefield's Rifle Volunteers

Anthony Leslie Dawson was born in 1980 at Manygates Maternity Hospital, Wakefield. He is a great-grandson of C H Drake, the founder of the Wakefield concern of Drake and Warters, shopfitters. He was educated at St John's, the Cathedral and Ossett schools before going on to Bangor University to read Archaeology and History. He has a keen interest in archaeology and in Napoleonic warfare. He worked as a volunteer from 1994-1998 on the Woodhall moated manor project. He is a member of La Garde Imperiale which recreated the Old Guard of Napoleon I. This has led to his interest in both Napoleonic volunteers in Wakefield and the Victorian volunteer soldiery. He is working on the life of Admiral Binstead RN.

8. FROM FARMS TO STAGE AND SURGERY: THE WOOD FAMILY OF CRIGGLESTONE AND WEST BRETTON

Tony Petyt was born in Wakefield and educated at Queen Elizabeth Grammar School. He then studied agriculture at Askham Bryan College, York, and on qualifying joined the staff of the college farms. In 1964 he obtained a managerial post with a large farming company near Morley which he held for the next seven years. In 1971 he decided to make a career change and became a residential social worker at the Henshaw's School for the Visually Handicapped at Harrogate. In 1974 he became a welfare officer with the Wakefield M D Council Education Department where he stayed until he took early retirement in 1996. He is the secretary of the Gissing Trust and is involved with the running of the Gissing Centre in Thompson's Yard, Wakefield. Apart from Gissing research his interests include local history, genealogy and book collecting.

9. THE HISTORY OF WEST PARADE METHODIST CHAPEL

Paul Dawson is the elder twin brother of Anthony and is currently reading History and Archaeology at Bangor University. He is a great-nephew of John and Jesse Archer, Cocoa Matting manufacturers and owners of Craven Mill, Westgate. He has always been a Methodist and is the fifth generation of Harveys and Cresswells to attend the now-closed Westgate End Methodist Chapel, where his great-great-grandfather, James Harvey, was for eighteen years the choirmaster and his grandmother was a chorister and, for a short period, organist. His interest in the Wesleyan Church in Wakefield stems from this background as does his love of the pipe organ; like his brother, he is a self-taught organist. He is currently writing a history of the Methodist Church in Wakefield.

10. SHOPS AND STREET TRADERS IN OUTWOOD

Norman Ellis was born and raised in Outwood, near Wakefield. He was educated at the village's Ledger Lane Council School and Rothwell Grammar School. After working for three years in Wakefield as an apprentice engineering draughtsman, he obtained a similar post at an Ossett firm where he stayed for thirty-nine years. He has lived in Ossett since 1960. Norman took early retirement in 1989 to concentrate on his leisure interests, the main one being local history. In addition to numerous articles, he has written over a dozen books, including ones on Wakefield, Dewsbury, Batley and Morley. Being especially interested in industries and transport, he has also produced studies on these. His writing relies heavily on old picture postcards, which he began collecting in 1970. He has also built up a choice collection of books and ephemera, which enables him to do much of the research at home. Other interests include photography and gardening.

11. WALTER HAMPSON, DIALECT POET

Peter I Wood was educated at Normanton Grammar School from 1944 to 1949 and served in the RAF before returning to work for a local engineering company. Later he went to Scawsby College of Education and then taught in Pontefract. He has been a member of Wakefield Historical Society and its council for over twenty years and is currently a vice-president. He has written and published a school history and the *Sandal History Trail*. He is currently involved in the preparation of a book covering Belle Vue, a district of Wakefield. He is involved with the U3A and walking groups and is very interested in local history. He has taken part in study days for schools and archaeology open days at Sandal Castle and has undertaken enactments there. He is married with a son and is a grandfather.

13. GIVING EFFECT TO THE DONOR'S INTENTIONS

Sue Lambert was born in 1962 at Eglin Air Force base, Florida. Her childhood was spent in Norfolk and Northamptonshire. She gained a BA (Hons) degree in History and United States Studies at Reading University. Her postgraduate diploma in Library and Information Studies was done whilst working in the Reading University library on day release at the North London Polytechnic. She studied on a part-time basis at Reading for an M Phil; her thesis on '*Seventeenth-century Berkshire Almshouses*' was completed, and the degree awarded in 1998. A career move brought her to Leeds in 1993 when she joined the cataloguing department of the British Library at Boston Spa. The main focus of her research is in almshouses and she has an interest, too, in non-educational charities.

14. HOLLIN HALL TRAMWAY, CLIFF COLLIERY AND THE CLIFF COAL AND FIRECLAY COMPANY

Keith Wainwright is the son of a mining surveyor and lifelong inhabitant of Crigglestone. He was educated at his village church school. Wakefield Academy, Highfields Grammar School and Whitwood Mining and Technical College. Employment for the whole of his working life has been in local government, initially in the County Mining Engineer's department of the former West Riding County Council, and subsequently with the South Yorkshire County Council and the Barnsley, Doncaster and Rotherham authorities' joint Mining Department, SYMAS. He was for some twenty years responsible for the compilation of a major archive of mining information covering the whole of the county of South Yorkshire. He is the author of numerous historical studies of Crigglestone and district and is presently researching the history and involvement of Crigglestone 'tommies' in the Great War.

INDEX OF PEOPLE

INDEX OF PLACES